Texas
in her own words

as told to
Tweed Scott

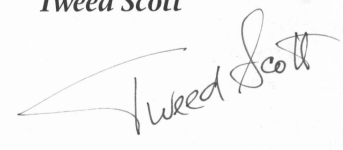

Redbud Publishing
Victoria, Texas

Texas: In Her Own Words
As told to Tweed Scott

Publisher: Sylvia and Steve Tomlinson, Redbud Publishing

Cover and interior design © TLC Graphics, *www.TLCGraphics.com*
Photo credit: Zee Chouinard

First Edition

ISBN: 0-9720293-7-0

Scott, Tweed
Texas in Her Own Words

Texas—History, local 2. Texas—Social life and customs 3. Texas—Biography
4. Interviews—Texas 5. Texas—History—Anecdotes

F 386.5 S442   976.4 Sc

Thank you, God for making this book and all things possible.
I never say thank you often enough.

To Whitney and Tyler, my children. It is a privilege to be your Dad.
Thank you for becoming the good people I have always prayed for.
You have both brought intense value to my life.

Zady, you have been a gift to me.
You are the wind beneath my wings and the lady who makes me possible.
I strive to be better—not for me—but for you.

A Big Ol' Texas Thank You

What started at the dinner table with a seemingly throw away remark evolved into an obsession-like quest. That journey led my wife and me to virtually every corner of the state, resulting in a little over 4,000 miles on what was then a new car. As you will see, we talked to some remarkable people. Had this book never been published, the effort would not have been wasted. The experience has been priceless.

The most enjoyable aspect of *Texas In Her Own Words* has been the undeniable privilege of meeting and talking with Texans no matter where or how I found them. This book about Texas was really written by Texans. I have merely served as the conduit for their words. They are the source of any value, insight or enjoyment you receive from this work. Their contributions are deeply appreciated.

Doing a book comprised mostly of interviews is comparable to herding cats. Finding and convincing people to sit down and spend time with you can be a daunting task. Although, I found, once I got people talking about Texas, they got into it. I did have some help in finding many of the contributors you're about to meet.

There are many people who have been instrumental in helping bring my dream to print. At the top of the list are Steve and Sylvia Tomlinson at Redbud Publishing. They saw the vision and felt my passion for this project from the first time they heard of it. We knew each other less than two hours when they told me they wanted to publish my book. At the risk of sounding somewhat giddy, my feet still have not firmly touched the pavement. They have not only been good partners in this endeavor, they have become cherished friends as well. Thank you for "buying in" and making my dream your dream.

Tami Dever, owner of TLC Graphics, designed the cover you are holding. She is a remarkably talented book designer who deserves every award she and fellow designer Erin Stark have ever won. She too saw the vision before she saw the words and pictures. Thank you for your unswerving support and believing in this effort. She has become a deeply respected and valued friend as well. Erin is responsible for the way everything looks between the covers. My heartfelt thanks for making us all look good.

> **I wouldn't trade the experience for anything in the world.**

When this book was just an idea, I attended one of Bobbie Christiansen's publishing seminars. It changed my life. I came away convinced that I could write a book—this book. Unbeknownst to her, she gave me the confidence and belief in myself. I knew the concept behind this book was valid. She started me on this journey. I wouldn't trade the experience for anything in the world. Bobbie, the RV is next.

I owe much of my writing dream to T.J. Greaney, the owner and publisher of *Countryline Magazine* in Austin. When I was about to retire from broadcasting, I was producing a weekly hunting and outdoor radio show. TJ was the host of that show. About a month before I left radio for good, I gave him a little piece that I had written called "The Real Deal" (it's here in the book). He liked what I had written and asked if he could put it in his magazine. I was blown away! He wanted to publish something I had written! The next month I was assigned a 1,200 word History of the Rodeo story. That was back in 2001. I've been writing for him off and on ever since. TJ, thanks for the encouragement and being a mentor.

Other thanks go out to Karen Jambon and Todd Schmidt, two colleagues I'm honored to call friends. There was a time when I worked for them. They provided the freedom and flexibility to rundown interviews as they became available. Many of the people gave next to no notice when they were ready to talk. When they spoke, I jumped (and was happy to do so). Mickey Rose, a good friend, has been an avid supporter throughout the journey. He's given me several good ideas since he first heard of the project. He's a native Texan who bleeds orange. (UT orange, of course!) Thanks for your many kindnesses and suggestions.

Mike and Andra Floyd have been friends going back to our radio days together in North Texas. They were instrumental in finding several of the Nacogdoches people. I could never adequately repay them for their friendship and hospitality. They have always been and always will be special people.

On the other side of Texas, Steve and Carla Kennedy run the Old Schoolhouse Bed & Breakfast in Ft. Davis. It was my intent to go out to West Texas and talk with some of the old pioneers. Carla put in me touch with several of the locals. The B&B was once a schoolhouse. Three of their rooms were named Readin', 'Ritin', and 'Rithmetic. Can you guess which room we stayed in? It was a great place to spend time in the majestic Davis Mountains. I not only want to thank them for their assistance but endorse their inn. It's a wonderful and peaceful place to hang out.

Rita Mills of Houston unwittingly made this book happen. She agreed to meet me in Austin to give me some ideas on how to find some creative financing for self-publishing *Texas In Her Own Words*. After we had talked for about an hour or so, we decided to go into the restaurant for dinner. When we got there she saw a couple of friends of hers and suggested that we all eat together. Her friends, total strangers to me, were my soon-to-be publishers, Steve and Sylvia Tomlinson. That is just a sample of the serendipitous things that have happened to make this book a reality. I could write a book on how the book became a book.

My mother-in-law, has always been an inspiration for me. Mary Catherine, an octogenarian, has always piqued my fascination of history. She has told me the story of her mother's journey to Texas in a covered wagon and how she lived long enough to see Sputnik in the night sky. I have often thought about all the unknown things her mother must have seen in her life. MC has shown me that hardy pioneer spirit while at the same time emanating the delicate qualities of a southern lady. One couldn't ask for a better role model for a Texan.

I owe my sister-in-law, Gaye, big time. Gaye allowed me to interview several of her Braum's customers in Canyon. She got me onto several other interviews in Canyon and Amarillo. I doubt I could have arranged them myself. Hugs to you, Gaye.

I also owe a debt of thanks to Kevin, my nephew, who had me talking to the Randall County Sheriff, Joel Richardson, in his office and not in his jail. Kevin also has always had a deep fascination for the weather. I knew I could count on him to hook me up with a meteorologist. All I had to do was ask. Thanks Kev.

Chris and Kim Copeland also had a hand in the Amarillo trip and saw to it that I got to talk to some other people too. Thank you for being you.

While we're still in Amarillo, thanks go out to Cynthia Taylor, the manager of the Soncy Road Starbucks for allowing me to talk to several of her willing customers and employees. Thank you for the coffee and the hospitality.

Speaking of Starbucks, a special word of appreciation is needed for Cheryl Arredondo and her crew, Linda, Jillian, Summer, Jon, Cat, Lorenzo, Jennifer, Jowell, Kassandra, Nick, Ken, Ryan, Jen, Doug, Anna Alicia and the rest of her cast at William Cannon and Westgate in Austin. Almost half of this book was written, edited, and sweated over in your store over the past two years. Thank you for letting me hang out in the corner at my favorite table and allowing me to become part of the furniture. Your many kindnesses have not gone unnoticed.

I want to thank Bobby Boyd, a true entertainer, for the deeply appreciated gift of the lyrics for two of his songs, "I Wasn't Born In Texas" and "The Ghost of the Alamo". Bobby found it in his heart to share some valuable time with me when it wasn't the easiest thing to do. He had recently lost his son due to a senseless crime in Nashville just weeks before. I know it wasn't easy. Bobby, your generosity and talent are boundless.

There is no way I could mention all the names of all the people who had a hand in making this project come to life. There has been constant encouragement from my fellow members of the Texas Writer's League and the Tejas Toastmasters. Thank you for believing in the work.

I also want to thank Zee, my wife, for the stunning picture that appears on the cover. The picture itself is a fluke. During the course of the researching and interviewing, we always had a camera within reach. One day after a brief storm, we headed into town. The weather was unsettled but clearing. As we drove by a Texas flagpole, some-thing remarkable happened. As we passed the flag, I noticed how the angle of the sun allowed it to pass directly behind the flag. The effect was breath taking. Although it washed out the hard colors of the flag, it resulted in an eerie effect. I told Zee, "You have got to see this" and I turned around and went back. She climbed out the

car and literally stood in the bar ditch and took two pictures. What you see on the cover is what came out. Little did we know that Tami, our book designer, would choose this picture for the cover.

I also need to thank Henry Williams, a great friend. He saved my life several years ago. When I needed a good friend, he was there. I'll never forget what he did for me. I would do the same for him in a heart-beat.

> I think that a case could be made for that thing we call the "Texas Attitude" or "Tex Appeal"...

Even though I interviewed him for the book, I want to express a special thank you to Paul Andrew Hutton. He was not only generous with his time but with his suggestions. He brought the article from the *Southwestern Quarterly* to my attention. "Stephen F. Austin's Bones" by Greg Cantrell was an absolute eye-opener for me. I might have found it on my own but certainly not as quickly. For me it was the "ah ha" moment of the project. After reading that scholarly work, it verified much of what I had learned. It was the proof I had been seeking. The marketing of Texas was not a quirk of social geography, it was intentional and deliberate. I think a case could be made for that thing we call the "Texas Attitude" or "Tex Appeal" having its roots in that process. Once the process of promoting Texas began, it was not hard to see how individuals might have become more willing to express their feelings of pride. There clearly is a nationalism of Texas. It is as real as the air you breathe. It's no secret it has been promoted and exploited for both public and selfish benefit for decades.

The amazing thing about writing a book is that so much of it is done alone and yet there are so many other fingers in the pie. As you read this book, recognize that you are listening to the heartfelt and deeply personal thoughts of the people who walk the talk in Texas everyday of their lives. Listen to their voices. It is through them that we can get an appreciation of the Texas psyche. It truly is unique. They are unique.

In closing, I have but one regret. Neither of my parents lived long enough to see this work come to life. My parents, Norma and Hal influenced me my entire life. I wished I could have shared this with them. They were good people. They made a huge difference in many lives besides my own. There was Chuck, Scott, Shelley, Briana, Ian and more than a hundred foster children over thirty something years. I'll forever be in their debt. Rest well. You've earned it.

Finally, I want to thank you for purchasing *Texas In Her Own Words*. More than that, I am humbled you have chosen to share your most precious commodity with me—your time. Feel free to contact me if you want to share your thoughts about Texas. There's a good chance we'll do this again. It would please me to include you in the next volume. I'd love to hear from you. I'm at the other end of *Tweed@TweedScott.com*. If we should meet somewhere in Texas, c'mon up and say howdy and I'll extend a hand. Again, from the bottom of my heart, thank you.

A Special Note of Thanks

Many serendipitous things have happened throughout the process of writing this book, not the least of which was meeting and working with Poodie Locke. I have known who Poodie was for years. I had attended shows at his Hilltop Bar & Grill enjoying the likes of Steven Fromholz, Mike Blakeley, the Troubadours, and Bobby Boyd. Poodie, as I had been told, is one of Willie Nelson's best friends and has served as the entertainer's road manager for years. When I met Bobby Boyd to interview him for *Texas In her Own Words,* Bobby suggested we meet at the Hilltop.

When we sat down to talk, Bobby introduced me to Poodie and asked if it was OK if he sat in with us. It was fine with me, some of the resulting conversation can be found elsewhere in the book.

During the course of the interview, we talked about several things, other enter-tainers, the Alamo, Texas, and notable Texans. He flat out told me, "You can't write a book about Texas without including Willie Nelson, Darrell Royal, and the Alamo." I told him I'd love to include them but they are not easiest people to get on the phone. He told me he'd set me up with them. He did. He also arranged to take me out to the "Alamo" movie set on Riemer's Ranch twice. This was before the movie was released. It was a breathtaking and awe inspiring site. (Some of the pictures are in the book). It gave me a real sense of what it must have been like throughout the 13-day siege.

On one of the trips out to the movie set, I expressed the desire to get Kinky Friedman, a respected Texas author and candidate for governor of Texas, to do the foreword for the book. Poodie provided his number. I called Kinky and he agreed to do it.

Catching up with Willie was a chal-lenge. On two occasions, I went to meet him on his bus prior to a couple of Austin concerts. Willie was under the weather and really didn't feel up to it. I understood and hoped for another day. When it came, I was under the weather and could barely get out of bed (I didn't need to give Willie what I had, whatever it was). There were a few other close calls, but finally Willie called me on his way to Dallas to catch a plane for Scotland. After playing voicemail tag and cell phone dropouts, we got the interview done.

None of this would have happened without Poodie's efforts. I told him I'd give him his own thank you page. I am that grateful for his help. He too saw

the vision of this book. It's better because of him. If you get down toward Austin and you want to see live country music, Poodie's Hilltop on Highway 71 West in Spicewood, Texas is a great little venue to catch a country show. It is absolutely true that you never know who may saddle up to the bar beside you—Willie, Billy Bob Thornton, Merle Haggard or whoever. It really happens there. While you're there, buy some of Poodie's barbeque sauces. They are good—really.

Poodie, thanks a million. You came through. Thanks for sharing your friends with me. I will forever be in your debt.

Foreword: Kinky Friedman

Tweed Scott wasn't born in Texas, but by writing *Texas in Her Own Words*, he's given many spiritual Texans a chance to enjoy what's great and unique about our state (hopefully, without getting here as soon as they can). Real Texans, spiritual cowboys, even people who thought they were bored with Texas history, are going to love this book. Now that I am running for Governor of Texas as an independent, Tweed's inspired efforts speak to me in an even more personal way. After all, this is the state Sam Houston fought for. It's the state Davy Crockett died for. *Texas in Her Own Words* and my campaign for governor have this in common: We are both searching for the soul of Texas.

Some of the people and places in this book are gone now, but their spirit remains as strong and vibrant as ever in this living chronicle of what it truly means to be a Texan. Some of the stories and interviews that follow are funny and some are sad and some are so redolent of the ragged-but-righteous spirit that built this state that they defy categorization. Above all, this book is entertaining and informative and as refreshing as it was to ladle a drink of cool water right out of the horse trough when you were a kid.

> A living chronicle of what it truly means to be a Texan.

Tweed Scott has done a great service to Texas. He might, I believe, even make a pretty fair Lt. Governor. But politics, of course, is never as important as people and places and the cowboy poetry of the heart. *Texas In Her Own Words* is chockfull of all of these things. It deserves a special place on your bookshelf. Say right between Larry McMurtry and J. Frank Dobie.

Table of Contents

Alphabetical Listing of Interviews

Watch What You Say, Podner

Texas: *In Her Own Words*, is the result of a throw-away comment at the dinner table. Let me explain. I was not born in Texas. Truth be known, I was born in Providence, Rhode Island and grew up in Laconia, New Hampshire. I enlisted in the U.S. Navy and the morning after graduating from Laconia High School, I went off to boot camp. I joined the Navy to see the world. Within a few months of boot camp, much to my chagrin, I found myself stationed in Kingsville, Texas, about 40 miles south of Corpus Christi. I was shocked. I didn't know the Navy was in Texas. I thought it had been reserved for the Army and the Air Force.

While stationed there I met a beautiful Texas native and we were married before my enlistment was done. I'll spare you the details of my life but let's hit the fast forward button some 30+ years. By now, life has taken its ravages.

My son, Tyler, was born in Austin, Texas. One hot night in July we were talking at the dinner table. I was gritchen' and complaining about something, as fathers will do on occasion. All I remember is that my wife, the lady from Memphis, Texas, turned to my son and said, "Tyler, don't pay any attention to your dad. Remember, you have something your father can never ever have."

"What's that?" he asked.

"You were *born* in Texas," she said smugly.

The words remain seared into my brain to this day. The first thing that flashed through my mind was, "How arrogant is that?" Then it hit me like the proverbial ton of bricks. These people are born with an extra gene! I swear to God, there must be a T-Chromosome or something. What is that all about? Where does that come from? I decided right there on the spot that I was going to make it my mission to find out. So I began asking Texans what makes Texas so special.

Moreover, if it applied to them, what does it mean to be a Native Texan?

Frankly, I was paradoxically surprised by both the diversity and the similarity of the answers. It wasn't long before I knew I was on to something. That's how this all started. From my previous travels around this huge state, I knew that Texas had several states within the state, so it was obvious that there was no way I could sit in my favorite coffee-house in Austin and write a book about Texas. I had to get out, go to every part of the state, and talk to the people who live there. That's what I did.

I trusted the book to tell me what I needed to know. I just had to do the work. I did and the book did its part. You need to know that I have long held a deep-rooted passion for my adopted state. That passion is even more profound after driving thousands of miles around the state and talking to her people. Through this process, several concepts began to take shape. See if you hear and see them too.

So Why Are Texans The Way They Are?

T exas is special.

Ask anyone who lives there or was born within her borders and they will tell you. There is a mystique about Texas that is as real as the air you breathe. Texans possess an innate sense of belonging to something special. They somehow know they are an intrinsic part of something bigger than themselves. You can see it in the way they carry themselves. There's a swagger in their step. It's as though they are born with an extra gene or chromosome teeming with pride and a "can-do" attitude.

The mere mention of Texas evokes a staggering array of images. No two people see Texas the same way in this land of contrasts and contradictions. The make up of her people is as diverse as the land they share. Blessed with a culturally rich heritage, Texas is a vivid tapestry sewn together by colorful characters and events. Her history encompasses a wide expanse, from the footprints of Spanish explorers on the shores of the Gulf of Mexico to boot prints of astronauts in the Sea of Tranquility on the surface of the moon. The journey in between is as fascinating as any story ever told.

Many things can be said about Texas. Some outsiders passionately express a hatred of Texas and Texans. Admittedly, some Texans can be insufferable. For the less enlightened, it is hard to comprehend how anyone can feel so good about where they're from or where they live. No doubt about it, there is plenty of justifiable pride to go around for each of our fifty states that comprise this wonderful country. But Texas? Texas is special. It's the people, the land and an attitude exhibited by both.

The people in this book are portrayed as precisely as possible. It has always been my goal to accurately capture the words and emotions of the contributors. Each

Texas is loved and admired because it is special to her people.

explains Texas in their own words and in a way only they can convey, without any interjection or editorializing from me. So if sometimes thoughts seem to wander or quickly jump from one place to another—enjoy it—you are eavesdropping on a personal conversation and this is the best way to capture the sense of who they are and the way they feel about Texas. To do it any other way would be less than credible.

The people you will meet between the pages of this book came from everywhere. Those whom I did not meet, shared their thoughts through e-mails and phone interviews. Most however, were face-to-face interviews.

You will soon experience the words of Texans. The people you'll meet come from all walks of life—some famous and not so famous, white collar, blue collar, native and transplant—each with their own understanding of Texas. They'll share their thoughts and emotions with you, and you'll learn that Texas isn't just a place to live. You live Texas. It's a mindset, an attitude, a sense of knowing that you are special. Texas is different. Texas is unique. Texas is an experience. Texas is a lifestyle.

The Lone Star state is only one of two states that was once its own country. The other state, Hawaii, was not a country but a constitutional monarchy that was later, under rather dubious circumstances, annexed. One indisputable fact remains—Texas fought for and gained its independence from Mexico. Texas is still a place where independence and freedom is cherished and admired. Travel where you might but you will not find anything quite like it. In his book, *"Travels With Charley,"* John Steinbeck said, "Texas is a state of mind. Texas is an obsession. Above all, Texas is a nation in every sense of the word." It's a fact. There has always been a sense of nationalism in this state. You feel it everywhere, even from the state's tourism slogan: "Texas. It's like a whole other country". Texas native Kenny Rogers expressed it in his 1989 song and video entitled, "Planet Texas." Now that's big!

There is no denying Texas has always been a land of stark contrasts. For within its expansive borders, you can find just about anything you can imagine. The Texas landscape is as diverse as her people. Both exude the image of this unique place. Even the weather runs between serene and majestically violent. Her people still possess an indomitable spirit that has legacies rooted seven generations back. They are Texas.

Texas is loved and admired because it is special to her people. Their forbearers created the legends and mystique that are Texas. Every one of them has their own stories and opinions to add about the place. It is my most passionate wish that you have an idea of why Texans are the way they are. They often cannot consciously tell you what it is that makes them genuinely and uniquely Texan. They don't have to. They feel it and intrinsically "know" what it is that they possess.

So who better to speak of her virtues? Listen closely to what they tell you. There is as much to learn between the lines as there is in the words themselves. So why are Texans the way they are? Settle back and let Texas tell you in her own words.

Texas on Hinges

unless you've been to Texas, it is really difficult to comprehend how large it really is. Its 254 counties take up the more than 276,000 square miles of wildly diverse geography. To get some kind of understanding of Texas' immensity consider the following:

If you were able to place door hinges on the four extremities of Texas, you would be amazed at how large Texas is in relationship to its neighbors. For example, if you could pick up Texas along its eastern border with Louisiana and Arkansas and flip it on a hinge mounted on the extreme western border at Anthony, Texas, west of El Paso, the Texas city of Orange would find itself in the Pacific Ocean south of Los Angeles and west of San Diego.

If you were to reverse that and pick up the point of extreme west Texas near El Paso and flip it, El Paso would be in the Atlantic Ocean east of St. Augustine, Florida.

If you were to lift the state at its southern most point at Brownsville and flipped it along the northern border of the panhandle, Brownsville would be 125 miles from Canada.

When you reverse that and pick up the panhandle and flip it over Brownsville, the northern border of the panhandle would be in the Pacific Ocean west of Guatemala and El Salvador.

HISTORY, HERITAGE and DESTINY

BILL ROBERTS

★ BIRTHPLACE ★
Manning, Louisiana

★ CURRENT RESIDENCE ★
Nacogdoches, TX

★ OCCUPATION ★
Teacher of Texas History

As I spoke with Bill and friends on a covered veranda of a big two-story
farmhouse in the country near Nacogdoches, a late afternoon thunderstorm
rumbled overhead. The lightning and thunder were relentless
but it didn't interfere with the conversation or the beer.

I think the whole historical background of Texas is what makes it different. Remember, we've been under the influence of six different countries. That has to have made a lot of difference. The French, the Spanish, the Confederacy, the United States and the heritage from each different one. There has been a wide variety of cultures.

We are all proud to be Texans. There is a mystique about being a Texan that is so hard to describe. It is something special to everyone here in Texas. Texas means something a little bit different to everyone who lives here. Go back in history and look at the massacre in Goliad, or the Alamo—these things are ingrained into the Texas psyche. It's always been there. Look back at the Spanish. They established the missions, even here in East Texas. All of a sudden we have the

There is a mystique about being a Texan that is so hard to describe.

French influence across from Louisiana and it's all together different. There was this influx of people starting with Stephen F. Austin when he brings these settlers in—300 families.

The history of Texas is so diverse, so much has happened here. The Spanish explored the coastline of Texas, there was the pirate Jean Lafitte who sat there at Galveston and who was pardoned for his efforts at the Battle of New Orleans.

It's hard to pinpoint what that all means. When you're a Texan, you have this independence. It goes all the way back to being a republic. I was born right across the Sabine (River) in Louisiana but still I consider myself a Texan. I lived here, basically, all my life. All my children were born here. There is a mystique about Texas and don't doubt for a minute that it isn't real. It sets you a part. It has to do with the independence that correlates with being a Texan.

It is the only state to enter the union by treaty and not the regular territorial annexation process.

DAVID STEWART

★ BIRTHPLACE ★
San Antonio, TX

★ CURRENT RESIDENCE ★
San Antonio, TX

★ OCCUPATION ★
Director of the Alamo Shrine, San Antonio, TX

David met my family and me in front of the Alamo Shrine on a warm July morning.
He was kind enough to give all of us a personal guided tour of the Alamo.
After the tour, we retired to his office nearby to discuss his job and Texas.
We sat under an original portrait of Sam Houston, which was hung directly
over a chair that once belonged to the Former General and President of Texas.
I can still feel those eyes staring at me from the portrait. Can you imagine working everyday
on the very same ground where Crockett, Travis, and Bowie died and
knowing that you're responsible to maintain the integrity of this hallowed place?

Texas is a very unique thing. My wife teaches Texas history, seventh graders—the first two weeks of her class every year talks about why Texas is special. And why it's special to be a Texan—because it really is—at least to us. It's got an absolute history of what freedom and fighting for freedom is all about—and struggling to keep the things that are important to

you. I spent 25 years in the military and I lived everywhere but I got back to Texas as fast as I could. I was a lot like Crockett, you know, "You can go to Hell. I'm going to Texas." It's really so hard to describe.

When I came to this job, my old boss just could not understand why I would want to do this. Finally I said to him, "It's a Texas thing." I'm not just going to a job, I'm going to a job that is part of my heritage. It is a job that relates absolutely to the sacrifices that my family has made here since 1837. To live in this beautiful state where you're free and have a special place in the history of the world—fabulous! People come

You can go to Hell. I'm going to Texas.

from everywhere to visit the Alamo because of what it is and what it represents. The battle that took place at the Alamo was not a unique battle—it has taken place all over the world in various and sundry times—in the 1500s in Japan and in Scotland at Abroth in 1320—the same thing took place. Ordinary men did extraordinary things for the cause of freedom. But I guess that gets etched on our souls when we're born as Texans.

We laugh about that. We spent 25 years in the military but all of my children are native-born Texans. That was very important to us. So we always managed to get back to Texas—or at least get my wife back to Texas—so they would be native-born Texans. It is so hard to put your finger on it but it's like another gene—to be a Texan.

I always say I'm a Native-American. That's because my family lived in Texas before it was a state. That heritage goes back all the way to the east coast when they fought the American Revolution. They fought for the same freedoms that the people in the Revolutionary war fought for.

From what I read about where I grew up down near Matagorda, where the Colorado River comes out into the Gulf, the people were not only pioneers, in a sense they came here to find a new life. But they were so giving of what they had and what they struggled for and

willing to share with their neighbors. I guess that's why Texas became known as a friendly state. That was part of the culture. You took care of your neighbor because it was the right thing to do. So many people came here from so many countries and stayed because of what was here and the attitude.

We recently had a gathering here that was really special to me. It was the Reserve Southern Special Forces Group that went to Iraq in September. They requested a Texas flag that had flown over the Alamo. So we sent them the flag. They came back and presented the flag back to the Alamo with a citation from the unit at their firebase "El Alamo" in Iraq. To me that is a very touching thing. They wanted that flag because they were proud of being Texans.

PAUL ANDREW HUTTON

★ BIRTHPLACE ★
Germany

★ CURRENT RESIDENCE ★
New Mexico

★ OCCUPATION ★
Historian, Documentarian

I will readily admit to being an avid viewer of the History Channel.

I recently watched a show about Daniel Boone and David Crockett.

Toward the end of the Crockett segment, Paul Hutton appeared to explain some of the

facts of the Crockett story. I remember thinking, "Crockett got it. He understood what

Texas was about." At that very moment, I jumped up and looked Paul up on the Internet.

I found an e-mail address and wrote him. I heard back from him in about ten minutes.

I was impressed. He said he'd be happy to talk to me about Texas,

one of his favorite subjects. It was good to get a point of view from a historian.

I think Texans have always had a larger than life attitude about themselves. Part of that simply comes from the geography and the landscape in which they live. Part of it comes from their history, which is romantic and unique, and part of it comes from the fact that they were a nation of their own for ten years of which they are very proud. That gave them a sense of separateness from the rest of the country even though they see themselves as the most essential of Americans. In their own minds they are the epitome of what it is to be American, yet they see themselves as somewhat of a special breed. All Americans have a sort of sense of exceptionalism, but Texans have taken that to the next level.

Texas was always a place of fabulous possibilities And the people who came here wanted to remake themselves in this new place and it didn't matter whether they came to here from Tennessee, Alabama, or Indiana, or whether they came here from central Mexico or Sonora. That still goes on today. People are seeking something in Texas. It has continued to attract newcomers throughout the centuries. That's one of the things Texas offers no matter whether you're coming from the South to the North or from the East to the West—you have the possibility of becoming something new. The current incumbent of the White House is a classic example of that. While his father is identified as an Eastern patrician, George Bush, the younger, has completely embraced Texas. No one would argue that he's not a Texan.

Texans pride themselves on the difficulty of their history. In that sense, I don't find Texas history more unique than many other places. A lot of people went through periods of travail and struggled to build something for future generations. But Texans had more space to act out their dreams than any other people here in the lower forty-eight. And so there was a sense, I think that they were somehow tougher, somehow a bit more wedded to the land and to both the beauty and the harshness of the land. The people were tempered by the experience.

The West is expansive. Vista is part of the Western heritage. Remember, for a lot of people, Texas was the first great west. And then it just kept going. While the landscape of East Texas would be familiar to folks from Tennessee and Arkansas on the Mississippi, the landscape of West Texas is foreign. The broad plains, the deserts of the southwest, the Big Bend country that was a new territory that Texans just adapted to. In their own minds it was tamed by the six-shooter and barbed wire.

They all share this sense of identity. You can bond the Hispanic Texan in El Paso with an oil worker in Houston—they share this common sense of pride in being Texan. That bridges this sense of community and who we are that transcends ethnicity, transcends class, transcends gender—it really is remarkable. And it's worked very well. That's one of the things, Texans have really bought into a shared identity, which gives them a unity that's the same thing that Americans have. In the United States we are disparate and different kinds of people but we share certain values that unites us North, South, East, and West.

> ## Texas was always a place of fabulous possibilities.

The main value that Texans share is this remarkable sense of identity. No matter who you are you are a Texan. This is especially true since the Civil Rights Movement and the change in the political status of black Texans and Hispanic Texans. The opportunity to identify oneself as a Texan and be proud of it has opened up even more so.

I lived in Texas when I was young, but mostly I grew up in Indiana, so for me if I were to go overseas I would say I'm from America. No Texan would ever say that. The only other state in the Union that I think has that sense of identity is Utah because of Mormonism. The Texans don't use religion (to identify themselves)... their religion is their identity.

Texans are very intense in their teaching of Texas. I got a good dose of Texas history when I was there and it has certainly stayed with me. I'm still doing Texas history, even though I don't live in Texas. My wife is from San Angelo. She has a clear identity of a Texan. So that makes her insufferable at times but there's a charm to it. The Texan has almost become a stereotype—a larger than life stereotype. There is a real love-hate relationship between the rest of America and Texas—which is exacerbated today on the political scene. The same sort of comments played out when Lyndon Johnson was president. Unlike Bush, Johnson was a larger than life person who just exuded, on purpose, I think, his "Texaness." He made everybody wear cowboy hats when they came down to the ranch—that sort of thing. He loved that image of himself. He was a Hill Country boy who pulled himself up by the bootstraps and became president.

I think indeed you do find with a lot of people a sense of putting down roots in Texas. If Texans do have to move out, it is with a sense of sadness. Texas is a place most people move into and what is very interesting is how quickly everyone embraces that image, you know, that idea of being a Texan.

Demographic change and the phenomenal growth came back in the 1970s. People moved out of the rust belt and moved down to Texas. The incredible growth around Dallas, Fort Worth and Houston. And the growth around San Antonio, particularly in the 1980s. These people very quickly embraced the idea of being Texans. I remember one of the state legislators proposed "Native Texan" be placed on special license plates that you could buy if you were born in Texas in order to differentiate the real Texans from all the Yankees moving in—the Yankees who of course changed the entire political structure. He was hooted down by people pointing out that Davy Crockett and Sam Houston would not have been able to get such a license plate.

———— ✦ ————

Texans made a very wise decision to identify themselves with the West and thus with the future. By identifying with the West, you identify with freedom rather than identifying with the South in identifying with slavery. By identifying with the West, you're identifying with success rather than identifying with the South and defeat. There has long been a debate among geographers and others as to whether Texas is a part of the West. For someone who was raised in San Angelo, I never had any doubt that Texas was part of the west. Others still see it as part of the South. Even when Texas was part of the Confederacy, they were freelancing. They were fighting their own war. Even if the Confederacy had been successful, I don't see Texas staying with it. Had that been the case, Texas just would have expanded West and formed its own country. I have little doubt of that. They did not have a strong community of interest with the slaveocracy and aristocrats.

Texas is a place that has embraced a self-image that's larger than life. What can you say about a place that has Lyndon Johnson, Davy Crockett, Barbara Jordan, Kinky Friedman and Willie Nelson. It just boggles the mind. Texas is full of characters. Everyone's always loved that. When John Nance Garner, "Texas Jack" Garner was vice president of the United States, people just went nuts back East. They loved it.

The Lone Star on Texas flags go back as far at 1819. Several flags with a single star were used as a part of the Long Expedition in 1819, the Austin Colony in 1821, and several flags of the early Republic of Texas. The familiar present day Lone Star flag was adopted in 1839.

MIKE HARRIS

★ BIRTHPLACE ★
Smithville, TX

★ CURRENT RESIDENCE ★
Bastrop, TX

★ OCCUPATION ★
State Trooper, Texas Department of Public Safety, Capitol Detail

Living in Austin, I will take almost any excuse to go to the capitol building.
I first saw it in October of 1968, and to use the vernacular of that time,
I was "blown away." Several years ago I wandered in and noticed a Texas Highway
Patrol Officer explaining the rotunda to some tourist. I saddled up close and
was completely taken in by his enthusiasm. This man absolutely loves his job.
He is without a doubt one of the state's finest ambassadors.

I explain the seals in the rotunda floor to tourists and tell them that Texas was an independent nation. One man said, "that's it!"

"That's what, sir?" I asked.

"That's why y'all are the way you are."

I said, "Basically, yes sir."

Texas is many states combined into one. The way I explained it to my cousin in Kentucky when he asked, "What is Texas like?

I asked, "What part?"

"What do you mean?" he said.

You've got West Texas where there's desert and some cropland. You have the high plains of Texas, in the Panhandle, which is mostly crop and some ranchland. You've got East Texas, which is nothing but a huge forest—big stands of pine trees, oaks and the rolling hills. Then you have Central Texas, which is scrubbier, but it has rolling hills and a lot of rock formations. And you have the coastal plains, which is where you'll find farming and ranching, and the coastline, so what part do you want to know about?

It was hard for him to understand that you have all this in one state. Remember, he's from Kentucky where it all looks the same.

I think the other part is that Texas was an independent nation before it became a state in 1845. That is something Texans really hang on to. We are special because none of the other states have that distinction, which is probably why you don't hear people walkin' around humming their state song but you will hear people in Texas do that quite a bit. You can hear "Texas" when my telephone rings. Saying you were born in Texas—you're special. You get that from childhood. I got it from my parents. It was something extra special because it was history. Because people came from all over to build Texas—that spirit is common still, from generation to generation. Texas pretty well sees itself as all-powerful, all-seeing and all-knowing. If you don't believe that you just be here and talk to one of us to find out about it.

⊷⊷≡⊷⊷

Texas really hasn't been an easy place to live. Just because something works in East Texas doesn't mean it's going to work in West Texas. They are so diverse. It was a hard place—there was, obviously, nothing here and the pioneers, they did the same thing in other states as well, but you had to be pretty hardy to come here. You might have come in with the Stephen F. Austin Colony and carved out a piece of your own in the middle of Mexico. You had nothing and no place to go get it. You just didn't send to St. Louis and get something on the railroad or by wagon train. You couldn't make it alone, which is why a lot of these little small towns you see are so close together. You didn't live that far apart because you did have to have your neighbor. With travel by horse, mule or wagon, you had to be pretty close. You had the Indians and the Mexican bandits to contend with, as well as some ne'er-do-wells that came to Texas. It was a big frontier.

Even Davy Crockett was looking for a new start, not just the next fight but he felt like his life in Tennessee had run its course by not being reelected to Congress. He came here looking for a new place to reinvent himself, relocate his family and take up the fight for Texas independence. We had people coming from all over. There were several countries represented at the Alamo, which I also think is a bone of contention with some of those peoples because they're not really given the credit they deserve—even the Mexicans that fought against their countrymen for Texas independence. I think a lot of them don't think they get the credit that is due to them.

People that were hearty in spirit and soul came here looking for that new start, looking for that land of opportunity. They got here, carved it out and built a magnificent place. Just ask any Texan.

To be a native Texan—that's a question I've really been trying to answer myself. It is something I feel. It's a part of my spirit. It's really hard to put into words. It's just knowing the stock I come from—I'm only like fourth generation Texan. Obviously, there are some families that have been here somewhat longer. Your parents do not only preach the greatness of Texas to you, but it's taught in school. We had such a colorful history from following the Mexican government to gaining our independence. We joined the Confederacy in the Civil War. A lot of people even wonder if Texas might still be an independent nation if we didn't keep having trouble with Mexico. But they kept making forays back into Texas and if it wasn't for the protection of the U.S. government at that time, I don't know if we would have joined at all. It's got a huge economy now. But they really needed the security then. It's really the only reason I can see why Texas even joined the United States back then.

Texas pretty well sees itself as all-powerful, all-seeing and all-knowing. If you don't believe that you just be here and talk to one of us to find out about it.

Starting in Elementary school, you start to get taught Texas history. The teachers who teach it, teach it well. It's pretty much pounded into you from day one.

I think it may be about that T-Gene or chromosome you're looking for. As for the pride, look at the state, look at what it does, look at what it has done. It's really easy to see why people would be proud of this state. People come from all over the world just to see Texas. They will visit the U.S. just to see Texas. The people—you can't keep 'em down—good economies, bad economies—the people work hard. That's maybe inbred too. Look to the people that came here first and started building it. We tamed it. Like West Texas or the Panhandle, the Cherokee Indians ruled and the Apaches ruled, the hearty people moved out and worked hard to make a livin' out of next to nothing. I don't know if I could but they did.

I wonder if Texas pride comes from the fact that we had to give up so much land when we became a state. Besides in Texas, you're the ruler of your own realm too. Land rights, water rights—water is the new "black gold" in Texas. Obviously because there's so little of it and everybody needs it. Twenty-two million people need it in some form or another. I wonder if that's also a big factor in why we got to keep all of our public lands. Texas is the only state that was able to do that. It's funny how when you go to say, Colorado and New Mexico and you'll see signs "Bureau of Land Management". The federal government, I think, owns more of a lot of those states than they (the states) do. Here it's ours. People will say that they come from a state that has 17 or 18 counties. They ask, "How many counties do you have here?" We have 254 counties. "My God! Well, this is a big place." They'll look at you dumbfounded too when you explain to them that we traded three million acres of land to pay for this capitol building—that was 10 counties in the Panhandle. They cannot fathom that. I do a tour for some German police officers every year about August. I finally did the conversion to Hectares so they could understand what I was talking about, I think it was 1,214,000 hectares and some change and their eyes got huge. I don't know how much bigger Texas is than Germany, but it's got to be bigger.

Everyone wants to own their piece of Texas. What runs on it, under it or through it is yours too, isn't it? This place amazes people from all over the world. For many of them that come from Russia, or the Ukraine, or the European countries, this is their focal point—the place they want to get to. I guess a lot of them expect us to be on a horse. Of course, they see our cowboy hats—part of the uniform—and our cowboy boots. That must solidify their thoughts about us! It's all about the cowboy image. They will walk up and point—"Hey there's a cowboy right there." Or they think you're a Texas Ranger—something they relate to. President Bush, in one of his speeches one time, said that if an American citizen is in Europe somewhere visiting and somebody in say Switzerland says, "Where are you from?" Texans don't say we're from the United States. We say we're from Texas. They relate to that. They understand what you're talking about. I guess truly deep down in my heart as much as I love the United States of America—I volunteered to go to Vietnam—if I had to choose between fighting for the United States or fighting for Texas, I'd fight for Texas first, I guess. I don't know if you'd do that for other states.

It's so engrained. Perryton, Dumas, or even Houston or Dallas—they're just a small part. The total is greater than all the parts. There is an old saying that you should never ask a man if he's from Texas because if he's not, you don't want to embarrass him.

I like those ads that Tim McClure did because Texas is like a whole other country. I'm surprised you don't have to get a visa or passport. I gave my uncle in Michigan a Texan card. My aunt drove him down here so we had to get him, at least, recognized as being a resident alien.

Somebody asked me one day about the word "y'all". Good word by the way. So is that singular or plural? I said, "Yes." It's universal. Y'all can be one. Y'all can be a hundred. Like the word "fixin'." I

thought that was proper English. Let's face it, there are folks who are not as fortunate as we are to live here.

It's something I feel. It's something I feel everyday. My pride certainly shows when I tell people about the state when they come here. It's part of my job but I can't help it.

I believe I was born for this job [working in the capitol building]. I like law enforcement. I liked bustin' crooks but now I get to work in the second most magnificent structure in the whole United States, the first one being the Alamo. You never have to tell a Texan to take his hat off in there either. There is a lot of history. A lot of great people have come through here. I just feel so fortunate to be able to walk the same halls as they have. I get to meet people from all over this world. I've met presidents of the United States. I've met tourists who spent every nickel they had to come to the United States and everyone in between. I can talk to them. I get a chance to brag about Texas to them. At least once a day or so, somebody will say, "Well, you're extremely proud of this place and this state aren't ya?"

"Does it show that much?"

"Yeah, it pretty much does.

Well, we're gonna tell our friends about you."

> I liked bustin' crooks but now I get to work in the second most magnificent structure in the whole United States, the first one being the Alamo.

They get to meet the big ol' cop they wouldn't normally talk to unless they're getting' a speedin' ticket or have done something. It's still that Texas pride. I want everyone to know we're not so bad after all. We have a human side too. God forbid they ever take me out of here.

If you were to drive from Brownsville, down at the southern tip of Texas to Texhoma, the northern most town at the top of the panhandle on the border with Oklahoma, you would have driven 862 miles. If you were to drive on Interstate 10 from Orange on the eastern border with Louisiana to Anthony, Texas on the western border with New Mexico, you would have driven 851 miles. Using that as criteria, Texas is 11 miles taller than it is wide.

MARSHALL KUYKENDALL

★ BIRTHPLACE ★
Austin, TX

★ CURRENT RESIDENCE ★
Outside of Driftwood, TX

★ OCCUPATION ★
Ranch Real Estate

When Stephen F. Austin began bringing in the "Original 300" families to Texas,
Marshall's ancestors were three of the first five families of that historic group.
He is tied directly to the land. In fact, that's what he does for a living.
He sells large ranches. He is the quintessential Texan. He looks every bit the part too.
He's tall with a distinguished mustache. He's a straight talker and you
just know he is a man whose word is his bond.

On my way back to my office, I setup the tape to listen to the ninety-minute interview.
The tape was blank! My heart sunk. In all the years I have been interviewing people
that had never happened to me. I was crushed. I immediately wrote him an e-mail
and apologized profusely over and over. He wrote me back and asked,
"Exactly how much forgiveness do you need?" He was gracious enough to let me
come to his house near Driftwood, Texas and do it again.
He has become a good friend. He's working on publishing his family's history.

I've read stories where people are six and seven and eighth generation Texans, when I look back there's no way they can be all that, I guess I'm about fifth. My fifth great grandfather was born in Kentucky but came to Texas with Stephen F. Austin so I do claim about five generations. The Kuykendall family is the great American story of travelers. We came into North Carolina way before the Revolutionary War. We were North Carolinians who came into Texas in 1821 but then some of my family members were born in Tennessee as my family came through there. So we're from that area for a hundred fifty years. My family came to Texas in the fall of 1821.

Three original Kuykendalls, who were brothers, were with Stephen F. Austin—Abner, Robert and Joseph. Actually the Kuykendalls were in the first group of five families of the "Old 300" (300 Catholic families) to cross to the west side of the Brazos River on the evening of the 26th of November, 1821. Stephen F. Austin met them over in what is now Austin County shortly after the first of the year. They were camped on a creek New Year's morning. So Abner called it New Year's Creek. It's just sorth of Brenham in Austin County. Austin came there to visit them. In the next year or so, Austin appointed them as captains of his so-called militia. Militia, from the American standpoint, the North Carolinians and Tennesseans, which is where it all came from—when the Indian trouble would come about,

people would send out the messages and they'd all get on horseback and all go chase the Indians. It was a rather family oriented militia but they would elect captains. For some reason, Austin appointed both Abner and Robert as his militia captains for the first part in the infancy of the colony.

All the "Old 300" were given a league and labor (pronounced La-Boor). (A league is 4428.4 acres and a labor is 177.136 acres.) The Spanish leagues—remember, we were then a part of Mexico because they had declared their independence in 1810—were all cut up the same way. All tracts of land had to go to water. So anything that was drawn up in those days was drawn to some body of water or some stream.

When old man Moses Austin got his concession in the early winter of 1821, he had his horse stolen from him. He walked most of the way into Nacogdoches in the weather of February of 1821. He got pneumonia and almost died. For whatever reason, he was a man who did not carry firearms and had no way to protect himself. I believe he walked alone. When he got into Nacogdoches, in one of the depositions I have found, he ran into Robert and Joseph Kuykendall on the streets of Nacogdoches and told them that he had gotten a concession for three hundred families in Mexican Texas. He then went back up to Missouri where he died shortly thereafter of pneumonia. His son, Stephen F., who lived in the Arkansas territory, reluctantly took over the job of moving these families. It was a real estate venture. Moses

Austin had been a very wealthy man; however, he lost all his money in the bank crash. It's now called the "Panic of 1819." He had lost his fortune. So he had come to Texas, as an old man, to recoup his fortune.

In the meantime, the United States government moved the first group of the Choctaw Cherokee. Now this is not the Trail of Tears which is about the 1830s, this is the early movement of the Choctaw Cherokee people from what we know as Mississippi, on the east of the Mississippi River to west of the river. They moved them into Arkansas territory. If you take Arkansas as a rectangle running north and south with the east side of it being the Mississippi River, they just went up in the northeast corner of Arkansas and drew a line southwest of there to the Red River, which would then be Mexican Texas. They said the Indians belonged on the northwest side of that. The Anglos belong on the southeast side of that. Our family was scattered all over northwest Arkansas into what is now Oklahoma territory. They had their cabins there and traded there. The army came in there and moved them out forcibly and burned their cabins down. All of these early settlers of the Missouri territory in Arkansas had moved down to Washington, Arkansas and along Pecan Point on the ridge just above what is now Mexican Texas. They were wondering what the heck they were going to do when Stephen F. Austin showed up and said, "We've got a concession for three hundred families." Boom! They were in Mexican Texas in a heartbeat. My family was there ahead of them and I've never found out why Robert and Joseph were in Mexican Texas because you had to have a passport to come into Mexican Texas in those days. They were here that early.

In the first *Handbook [of Texas]*, that was published in 1952, it says that Robert had been scouting previously in Texas. I don't know where they found that out. In one of the Maribeau B. Lamar (2nd President of the Republic of Texas) statements that I ran across, he had a deposition from Joseph. Lamar was collecting Texana materials in his later years. In the end his personal papers was a deposition by old man Joe Kuykendall who said they were on the streets of Nacogdoches when Moses Austin stumbled back into town and told them about the concession. So they just whistled up their brothers and their families and got with some other people, (the) Gillilands and some others and that's why they were in with the first five families. Immediately thereafter, the balance of the old 300, actually, there were 294, gradually trickled down over the next year or so.

> The Kuykendall family is the great American story of travelers.

I saw John Wayne in *The Shootist* the other night. It's the early part of the movie and he's saying something like

I just believe that you can take any state but people who are ranching people that are connected to the land have an attitude and a relationship with the land and what they have done with it and what it's done for them.

he's never laid his hands on another man and he doesn't allow people to lay their hands on him. That's funny how a character is developed around certain attitudes. People who are ranching people and are connected to the land have an attitude and a relationship with the land and with what they have done with it and what it's done for them. But also I think it has to do a lot with privacy too. A man's land in the United States is private, so if the people in Texas have larger ranches, perhaps some of them did and some of the them didn't, but in the early days, of course, our family got the leagues. Still it doesn't matter what size. I think a man has feelings that he can go on a piece of land that is his and that you cannot take it away from him. It is where he can grow into what ever he is going to be and whatever the land is going to do with him. I mean the land plays a big part in that. It just happens that my family is a family of landowners. We all have had land ever since we came to Texas, and before, with Stephen F. Austin. We've never migrated into doctors and lawyers and other things. We've basically always been landowners. If you were a landowner before the civil war, you were either a farmer or a rancher. We were ranchers not farmers. We didn't plow the ground, we raised cattle on it. So we came through the early stage of the cattle industry and the trail drives to Dodge City. We were very active. My family comes through that so-called Western heritage during that era of our country. When you look back, it's so much fun to think about and know about and write about, and know that you descend from these people who have been on the land and fought the Indians and did the *Lonesome Dove* stuff. I think the land is very much your identity. Because it shapes your outlook on how you function in the society you know.

Why did my family not continue to move? At that time, Americans moved west to the Pacific until they couldn't move any further. The people who came to Texas seemed to stay, by and large. I think it was because, as a nation now, we were a land of land traders. We've been in the real estate business since the first day we got here in the 1600s. We were out buying or getting a piece of land or trading for it or trading the Indians out of it—remember we came down the normal migration trails. Think about it, people took the Oregon Trail. They went out there for land. So Americans during that time of manifest destiny, or whatever you want to call it, were out seeking a piece of land. They'd work on one for a while and use it up or get tired of it, or it would get too crowded and they would move on and get another piece. The history of America is moving from one piece of land to another. And for some reason, we moved down here to Texas. After all these hundreds of pieces of land we had over all those years, suddenly we get to Texas, and we stay. It must have been because the leagues of land were so immense to the culture of that time. Think about it, Robert Kuykendall comes off that 100 acres of land that he had in Arkansas. His dad, Abner had 100 and something acres in Tennessee when they decided to get on a keelboat and float down the Ohio to the Mississippi and these younger boys get to Texas. Then the Mexicans lay 4,428 acres on them. I think it must have been astounding to them. Also, the land was extremely productive. They ran lots of cattle, horses and hogs, so it must have been a paradise for awhile until the Civil War came on. I had forgotten about the Civil War, we were all confederates and lost. So when we get home in 1865 from the war, and the Federals moved in and took over during Reconstruction, they taxed us in American dollars and we didn't have a single dollar, so they confiscated all our land.

They broke up most of the Brazos River and Colorado River bottoms where all those big leagues were put together. Those were all farms before the Civil War with slaves. That's why the blacks lived along the Brazos river bottoms because that's where all the big farms were. But all those farms were broken. I'd dare say, they'd be mostly intact today if there were not for the Civil War.

~ ~

I see Austin's Colony as the premier, really first colony of Texas. I don't see the other colonies in that light even though they were active. Austin's Colony was in the heart of the very active farming and ranching area of the coastal plains of Texas. And I think that's why the people stuck. Can you imagine coming here—the wild cane that stood several stories tall expanded out several miles on either side of the Brazos and the Colorado River on the coastal plain. To the extent that you could not go through it at all except where the buffalo crossed. So the major towns that you know of today, Beason's Crossing (Columbus) and the others on the Colorado and the Brazos, are at old Indian and buffalo crossings where they had to bust through the cane break. In later years all the cane was burned out and turned it into farmland.

~ ~

It is a tremendous sense of pride for me to be a Texan. The fact that I am just lucky—it's just a matter of the luck of the draw that I am born into a ranching frontier family. I didn't come as a merchant or something else, I came in as in all the stories we talked about. I am from the old West. I come from everything that is the epitome of the old West. The cowboys and the Indians, the six shooters, my family lived all that, so as I get older, and I try to write some of the history about it, it is a tremendous sense of pride that I came from this fairly narrow group of people that settled in Texas. It colors who I am today.

It's strange, I've always been immensely proud that my family fought in the Civil War until a few years ago when someone told me what we fought for... Well, I knew everybody had slaves and I should have put more value on that but I was immensely proud that all four of my great-grandfathers fought in the Civil War. They all fought for the South. I thought that's what you were supposed to do. But I am proud that I come from all that background. I think that's what molded me, it is a molding device, that's what molded me into being who I am. I have a great deal of fun going back and talking about my own family. These were my people. I have a narrow history that I have shared with you today that I am extremely proud of and I think that's what made me who I am today.

AUTHOR'S NOTE: *There is much more to this interview than we could include in this volume. Marshall goes into a great deal more detail about his family's experience in early Texas. If you would like to read the full text go to www.TweedScott.com. Look for the Marshall Kuykendall link.*

Texas is larger than the smallest 15 states
and the District of Columbia combined with room left over.

REAGAN PATTON

★ BIRTHPLACE ★
Nacogdoches, TX

★ CURRENT RESIDENCE ★
Nacogdoches, TX

★ OCCUPATION ★
Sales Manager for Cell Phone Company

Reagan worked sound for many concert artists, including the Texas legend,
Stevie Ray Vaughn. The thing that really struck me about this conversation
was the forthright honesty. Reagan feels Texas down to his bone marrow.
Like many Texans, he has strong opinions and isn't afraid to say what's on his mind.
As I sat there listening to him, I kept thinking of a variation to an old joke,
"Beauty is only skin deep...but ugly goes all the way to the bone."
Listening to Reagan talk about Texas and his family, I kept thinking...
Pride may only be skin deep but Texas goes all the way to the bone.

To me I'm not an American. I'm a Texan. I think being a Texan is a lot more important than being an American. We're the only state that still has the right to secede if we don't like things the way they are. Texas has everything. It has beaches, farm land, mountains, everything you could want. It's like a huge community too. Wherever I go in the state of Texas, I always run into somebody I know or that knows somebody that I know. The most special thing about Texas for me is just that people are friendlier and more caring and nicer as a whole than any-place else I've been.

When I was on the road, in other countries, working with different artists, I'd have to announce my nationality going through customs. I'd always say Texan-and I still do. Texans are more accepted in more places than most Americans just because we're more polite even though we have eccentricities. There is a mystique about this place. They've made so many movies about Texas, Westerns that were popular everywhere but really don't portray Texas at all. But when you travel out in the world, well everyone wants to know, "do you have any oil wells, how many cattle have you got, how big's your ranch?" It's kind of fun. Myself, when I'm traveling away from Texas, like when I'm in England or other places in Europe, I want everyone to know I'm a Texan. I wear my boots and my hat because it opens doors for me. People respect you because you're from Texas.

I enjoy Texas for a lot of reasons, you know, but to me it's one of the most beautiful places in the world. All of Texas is beautiful if you acquire a taste for it. I even liked Kingsville and the brush country to an extent. It had some real natural beauty to it but it was just hottern' hell and the snakes were huge. I was bit by rattlesnakes six times by the time I was ten years old. Actually it's rare that rattlesnakes kill anybody unless a whole bunch of them bit 'em at once. You get real real sick but you come through it. They were just every-where in Kingsville.

My great granddaddy had a large ranch in South Texas, down around [the town of] George West. Made a million and lost it ten times back during the 1940s, 50s and 60s. He made it and lost it over and over again in the ranchin' business, which just happens unless they punch a bunch of holes in the ground and a bunch of oil flows out. But you know, he wouldn't give up that lifestyle for anything. It was what he loved. It was what he was born into. My mother's side of the family was all Reagans from South Texas. Fact is, I'm about the only one not involved in cattle and horse ranchin'. Everybody else in my family is still in it down there.

Yeah, I just hope that not too many people from other places figure out what a great place Texas is and move in and start changing things. Now if they move into Houston or Dallas that's OK. Austin's too crowded now too.

JERRY JERNIGAN

★ BIRTHPLACE ★
Newport, Arkansas (Raised in St. Louis, MO)

★ CURRENT RESIDENCE ★
Junction, TX

★ OCCUPATION ★
"Philsopher"

This is another one of the men I talked with on that veranda outside Nacogdoches
during that noisy thunderstorm. Although the conversation started with Jerry,
Reagan Patton and Mike Floyd also added a thought or two along the way.
Formality was never an issue that evening. I rolled the tape and they provided the insight.

L iving in different places in Texas is unique. Fort Worth is different than Austin. Living in Palestine and Nacogdoches and some of these little East Texas towns are different than Central Texas. Living in Junction is different than Austin. That's the unique thing about Texas. When you go outside the state people think Texan. Just like people do out-side the U.S. Don't tell 'em you're from the United States, tell 'em you're from Texas—you'll be treated better. I've learned that.

What I find that really strikes out at me, that stands out, is the love of the state by Texans. They have a unique love for this place and would still get out there and defend it. I find myself even after 25 years plus of living here—if I thought there would be an invader, heaven forbid, of Texas—I would be there. This state has grown on me that much.

But Texas to me, it's not just the state, Texas is an attitude, you know? The people—yeah, there's buttheads everywhere—but the Texans that I have hooked up with, especially over the last ten or fifteen years or so, are connected at the heart. They're pretty unique that way. They either really like ya or they don't like ya. I have been very fortunate.

My favorite place in Texas is a toss up between the Texas Hill Country and East Texas but I think the real reason is that most of my real good friends are in East Texas. Home is where the heart is so to speak. Actually, this is my home away from home on this very porch. Junction is about seven hours from here (Nacogdoches). They're calling it the backdoor to the Hill country but it's the gateway to West Texas—pretty unique in that aspect. It was the last area of Texas to get law enforcement. Texas Rangers and Buffalo soldiers were the only ones that were defending that area of Texas. Even a lot of the Buffalo soldiers were killed because they didn't want no damned soldiers hangin' around there. John Wesley Hardin was shot in Junction. He didn't die but somebody had the guts to shoot him. The last Indian uprising, as I recall, where they kidnapped white people, took place in Junction and Kerrville. Fredericksburg was unique because the Germans who settled it

were, I think the only people who ever kept a treaty with the Indians, which was why they were never bothered.

For me [coming to Texas] was a culture shock. Coming from St. Louis to Texas was one, but when I went from East Texas down to Fredericksburg and I met German cowboys, now that's a zoner. There's another thing I really admire and sometimes it goes unnoticed is that where would Texas be without the Mexicans and the Mexican culture? The two are inextricably connected.

> But Texas to me, it's not just the state, Texas is an attitude, you know?

"My great great-granddad was the first medical doctor in all of south Texas. He covered ranches all the way from Brownsville to San Antonio to Uvalde and had to ride a buckboard as a doctor. I'm also related to Col. Patton, he led nothing more than a squad of men—to the Alamo from Glen Flat, Texas which is here in Nacogdoches County; they were the last soldiers to join the Alamo," stated Reagan Patton.

"My family up here were the Pattons and in the family cemetery they have eight Confederate grave markers. They ran a riverboat up and down the Angelina River before it all silted in from tobacco farmin'. They ran down to the Sabine River to Galveston and New Orleans. They'd take tobacco and cotton from here and bring supplies back. Eventually they got into the general mercantile business. There was a story in the paper about ten years ago that our family has the oldest surviving retail business (in the state) in continuous operation since 1834. It started as a general store downtown to Nacogdoches."

— ❊ —

John Wayne, in almost every western movie he did, mentioned Nacogdoches. It's the oldest city in Texas. You can see the smuggler's trace that went around the town of Nacogdoches. The wagon ruts are still visible from all the smugglers coming from Louisiana on their way to San Antonio. The only law enforcement in the state at that time was right here. The killin'est sheriff ever in the history of the state was Sheriff Spradley in Nacogdoches. I forget how many men he shot. It was like the Wild West. The last place they had a public hangin' in the state of Texas was right here—right downtown on the square sometime in the 1900s.

Nacogdoches and San Augustine and this area of deep East Texas right through here to northern Louisiana—it is so different than the rest of Texas because it's kind like the Old South, culturally it's closer to the Old South. It was a shock to me coming here from South Texas when I was in high school. In South Texas race didn't matter. You had to get along with everybody because that might be the only help you got. But now people in Nacogdoches, those generations, have moved on and the prejudice is not so much here in my generation.

Davy Crockett pledged his allegiance to Texas right here in Nacogdoches. The people at the Alamo were there from all walks of life to start over, to find their fortune. Something a lot of people don't realize is how close the mission compound was to San Antonio. For two days Santa Anna burned the bodies of the defenders. The Mexican soldiers were thrown into the river and the people of Baxter had to fish the dead bodies out so they could get clean drinking water.

I've always been fascinated by the Alamo and Texas history. The first thing you do when you walk into the Alamo—you take off your hat because it is a shrine.

— ❊ —

San Antonio, TX

DOUG RAYMOND ROSE

★ BIRTHPLACE ★
San Antonio, TX

★ CURRENT RESIDENCE ★
Grand Prairie, TX

★ OCCUPATION ★
Minister-Teacher

Doug Rose is a man I have never met. He found my web site, www.TweedScott.com,
and shared his thoughts about the Lone Star state with me. He is typical of the people
I was fortunate enough to have crossed paths with along the way.
So many of the people we communicated with had interesting backgrounds
or spoke of family who have done something noteworthy.
He wrote eloquently and expressed the depth of his feelings about Texas.

Texas is a special place to hold on to your dreams. It is one special spot where dreams may take root and thrive and grow. What does being a Texan mean? It means no matter where you travel, everyone knows you. We were in Belfast, Northern Ireland last year and everybody knew about Dallas, Texas due to the reruns of the TV show with J.R.

My favorite place is my birthplace of San Antonio. It is rich in historic heritage with the romantic architecture of missions like the Alamo. I love Texas because of my rich heritage here. My uncle Noah H. Rose is the author-pho-tographer-producer of the book: Texas Album of Gunfighters. Our family also dates back to my second or third cousin marrying President Lyndon Johnson's second or third cousin in the 1800's. It gives me a special sense of accomplishment to know our family has had a part in the preservation of the great State of Texas.

My journalism career began in Thomas Jefferson High School in the 1960s when I won a contest sponsored by the Ford Motor Co. and was dubbed the Teen Journalist of the Year in San Antonio. My winning story was about my discovery of old Mosaic tiles in the school basement that were purchased to be used on the dome of the historic school with the Jeffersonian architec-ture, but [they] still stood there untouched after all those years. Being a Native Texan is special to me for many of these reasons. I currently write a reli-gious column for the *Grand Prairie Times* Newspaper.

One of the things that has always fascinated me about Texas
is the uncanny connection between explorers from two seemingly
different worlds. In 1528, Cabeza de Vaca, the first Spanish
explorer on Texas soil, was shipwrecked on Galveston Island.
Four hundred and forty one years later, astronauts based
roughly thirty miles away were traversing
the surface of the moon on the Sea of Tranquility.

DAVID TOMLINSON

★ BIRTHPLACE ★
Fort Worth, TX

★ CURRENT RESIDENCE ★
Houston, TX

★ OCCUPATION ★
Oil & Gas Landman
Alter ego A. K. A. "Super Texan"
An unofficial mascot of the Houston Texans

David is someone you just might put into the "Extreme Texan" category.
This native Texan not only loves his state and his heritage but he has developed
an alter ego. He is "Super Texan." He is an unofficial mascot of the Houston Texans
football team. If you go to any of the home games, there's a good chance you will see a
grown man in the stadium dressed as a red, white & blue bull with a cape. Extreme? Maybe.
Like many Texans he must share the philosophy: there is no sense in doing things half way.
David even named his first son after a Texas icon. And not to be outdone, Ryan's little
brother carries the name of two famous Texas towns as Houston Tyler Tomlinson.

T he Houston Texans have a contest each year open to the fans in search of the ultimate Texan fan. I've entered in the last two years. This past year I was one of the final six to be in that contest. I didn't win it but I came in second place, I understand. The main thing I got out of it was to lead the team out onto the field for the Atlanta game last year.

It's kind of hard to put into words what makes Texas special. To me it's like a country all by itself. I was born in Fort Worth, lived in Louisiana for eight or nine years early in my life and then moved back here. I've never wanted, for whatever reason, to live anywhere else. Texas has got everything. I'm huge into sports, of course. I love all the teams in Houston. That's also a reason why I wouldn't want to move anywhere. The people are friendly and diverse. Just the country itself has all the outdoor activities, water sports, hunting, and fishing you could ever want. Everything is here. There's not a real reason to want to go anywhere else. I'll tell you now, I wouldn't want to go anywhere else. I would do anything possible to never have to leave the state.

You have to be independent. Not a lot is given to you that's for sure. I think

that's something that may be different than some of the other states. The Texas attitude comes from a combination of a lot of things. Texas has anything anyone could possibly want. That's why they're so proud of their state. People come here from everywhere to find jobs, especially Houston. It's been growing for 40 years. It's unbelievable. I don't ever really hear of people leaving the state. Just people coming in.

I'm just proud of the fact that I was born here. I was kind of lucky I guess. My dad is from Oklahoma—but both of his parents were born in Texas—and my mother's from Louisiana. My daddy ended up in the oil business. One of my brothers was born in Louisiana. I'm just proud of it. It's really hard to describe. It's the heritage, the history of Texas and how this country came to be. The

Alamo and all that coupled with all the things you can do in Texas. And the big thing with me now and for the past fifteen years is pro sports—Houston pro sports. I'm glued to it and I don't know how I could live without it.

—※◆※—

I was a big Oilers fan. I guess about the last five years that the Oilers were here I was a season ticket holder, and probably for five years before that. I go back to the Bum Phillips, Earl Campbell and the "Luv Ya Blue" days. Just ended up loving it all. Of course, like most Oiler fans here, I was devastated when Bud Adams moved the team. I don't totally blame Bud Adams because a lot of it was the county and city politicians and the media. I followed them to Tennessee because I love pro football— I had to follow somebody. But as soon as I found out Houston was going to beat L.A. out for a team, that's when I realized that as much as I loved the Oilers, it was the team from Houston I knew I would follow. Right away, I just turned off the switch and got ready to become a Houston Texan fan.

As soon as they decided to name them the Texans, I loved it. A lot of people here didn't like it. I'm not exactly sure why. And I was so proud that Houston got to have that name. I think most people now have grown to love it too.

I would do anything possible to never have to leave the state.

—┼—

So they announced the name, team colors and the logo. Again, I just love that steer head. There was just something about it. And I just thought, "Wow! I'm an Aggie." Although I only went to Texas A&M for one year, I feel: "Once an Aggie, always an Aggie."

Once they announced the team colors and the logo, I started work on my costume. It actually took me a few months to decide what I wanted to do. Building it took another two months. The costume weighs about 20 pounds. I support the team as much as I possibly can.

—※◆※—

Getting back to Texas, I would not want to go anywhere else. It is just a wonderful state. The only recreational thing you cannot do in Texas is snow ski. I like the food too. I'm a big cook. I like chili, barbecue and chicken fried steak. The food in Texas is unbelievable.

One of the greatest baseball players, if not a great Texas legend, is Nolan Ryan. I named my first son Ryan after him. My wife went for Ryan because she would not go with my original choice, Earl Derrick (a reference to Earl Campbell and the Oilers)—I was still an Oilers fan at that time. That was back in '99. Earl Derrick. My wife said, "I don't think so!"

—※◆※—

JOEL W. RICHARDSON

★ BIRTHPLACE ★
Canyon, Texas (Raised in Panhandle, Texas)

★ CURRENT RESIDENCE ★
Canyon, TX

★ OCCUPATION ★
Sheriff of Randall County, Texas

*Joel Richardson is the Sheriff of Randall County. His jurisdiction includes
the cities of Amarillo and Canyon, Texas. We sat quietly in his office and
talked about life in the Texas panhandle. As we wrapped up our meeting,
he offered a list of things that strangers should know if they're think of moving
to Texas. He's fine tuned and updated them over the years but I can easily
visualize a grizzled ol' Texan "splainin" these simple facts to a tinhorn.*

It's the people of Texas that make it so special. For instance, look at the Panhandle. The Panhandle wasn't created beautiful as far as the landscape, the scenery. We have the most horrid winds in the world. We have two distinct seasons. It gets cold-cold and yet it gets hot. But the friendly people of the Panhandle are what set it apart from other places. You can't go somewhere that you don't run into friendly people. We have the most courteous, friendliest people. That is what makes us different.

Being a native Texan means being proud to be a Texan. That is part of our motto around here. Not everybody is fortunate enough to be born in Texas, but they get here as quick as they can. That's the mentality. If you are born here and raised here you know that you are proud to be here. There is some-thing special about Texas. What is it? I don't know but it is something that is in everybody that is here. You don't spend time in thinking about why. You just are.

In the Panhandle we are closer to five other state capitals than to our own. We sometimes think in the Panhandle that we are forgotten by our own state government. In fact, there is a story about the capital build-ing. When the building was built, they tried to trade the Panhandle to pay the architect. Most of the three million acres that were used to pay for the capi-tol did come from the Panhandle. It's

> Not everybody is fortunate enough to be born in Texas, but they get here as quick as they can.

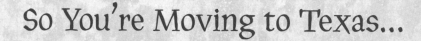

all been broken up and sold off. Agriculture was our mainstay and then oil. But not everybody in Texas is wealthy and not everybody wears a Stetson."

I think everybody in the Panhandle, whether they live in the city or not, considers themselves country people. No matter what or how hard you try to change it, it is still a network of good ol' boys. You do things to help your neighbor. You do things to help your community. You do those things. People around here are raised that way. It's easy to take advantage of peo-ple sometimes because of their good heartedness. There is a drawback to being that way, to being so open and good hearted—you can be taken advan-tage of by crooks. I've got something I wrote sometime ago and I have tweaked it and tweaked it over the years.

So You're Moving to Texas...

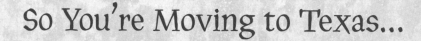

Here are a few simple rules and principles you should think about:

★ Pull up your droopy pants. You look like an idiot.

★ It's called a caliche road. I drive a pickup truck because I need to. No matter how slow you drive, you're still gonna get dust on your Lexus. Drive it or get out of the way.

★ So you have a sixty thousand dollar car. We're real impressed. We have a quarter-million dollar cotton stripper that we only drive three weeks a year.

★ They are pigs, cattle, and oil wells. No matter what they smell like to you, they smell like money to us. Get over it. Don't like it? I-40, I-20 and I-10 go east and west. I-35 goes north and south. Pick one.

★ Every person in a pickup waves. It's called being friendly. Try to understand the concept, and if you do it, use all your fingers.

★ We all started hunting when we were nine years old. Yeah, we saw Bambi, too. We got over it. Besides, "Bambi" taste like chicken.

★ If that cell phone rings while a bunch of dove are coming in, we will shoot it out of your hand. Don't have it next to your ear at the time.

★ Yeah, we eat catfish and crawdads. You really want sushi and caviar? It's available at the corner bait shop.

★ The "Opener" refers to the first day of deer season. It's a sacred day and falls on the closest Saturday to the first of November.

★ Any references to "corn fed" when talking about our women will get you jack-slapped (by our women).

★ We open doors for women. That applies to everyone, regardless of age, and the women here appreciate it.

★ No, there's not a "vegetarian special" on the menu. This is cattle country. Order steak. Order it rare.

Or, order the chef's salad and pick off the two pounds of ham and turkey.

★ When we put dinner on the table, there are three main dishes: meat, vegetables, and bread. We use three spices: salt, pepper, and Tabasco.

★ You bring "Coke" into my house, it better be wet, brown and served over ice. You bring "Hooch" into my house, it better have four legs, a tail, and have a nose for quail or pheasant. You bring "MJ", "Mary Jane", or "Mari—anything else" into my house and she better have long hair, a shapely figure and know how to drive a pickup truck.

★ Yeah, we have special flavorings of tea. It's called lemon.

★ The Lakers and Knicks may be special—but here Friday nights in the fall are sacred. It's called High School Football and it's a dang site more fun to watch.

★ Yeah, we have golf courses. Don't hit the water hazards. It spooks the fish.

★ Colleges here are not liberalism training academies. They are fine colleges. Graduates come out with an education and a love for God and Country, and they still wave at passing pickup trucks when they come home for the holidays.

* We have more Army, Navy, Marines, Air Force and Law Enforcement than any other state. We honor these men and women and only use them for back up. Per capita, each man, woman and child own at least two firearms and has taken some kind of NRA shooter education course.

* You is singular, y'all is plural. If we refer to more than that, it's all y'all. Y'all is a one syllable word. Do not stretch it into two.

* Just because you polluted the water and air where you came from, don't think you can do it here. If the grain dust in the air during harvest makes you sneeze, take an allergy pill. It's how we feed the rest of the world. Get over it.

* Our word is our bond. If you need a contract, it just tells us what to expect from you. Your handshake isn't worth spit.

* If we have to call on our law enforcement officers, get ready to have your butt kicked by the best.

The smallest state park in Texas is .006 acres.
It is the gravesite of Davy Crockett's second wife, Elizabeth.
It is located in Acton, just south of Granbury.

IN THE HEART OF TEXAS

TOMMY BIGGERS

★ BIRTHPLACE ★
San Augustine, TX

★ CURRENT RESIDENCE ★
Nacogdoches, TX

★ OCCUPATION ★
Sales Manager of Car Dealership

Texans love where they live. They realize the state is very large but they have placed their roots into their own locale. Although Tommy talks about Nacogdoches, other Texans bring the same enthusiasm to their own towns or cities.

Texas is the biggest and the best. It's the best state to live in. Now, it is the only state I've ever lived in. The weather's great. The people are great. It has a great reputation and a great heritage. In talking about East Texas, it's a good pace of life. You get down home people. Everybody gets along very well. We have a nice quality of people. Weather is one of the things we really like about it. The East Texas lifestyle is a slower pace. Nacogdoches has a population of about 35, 000 people. You can get the kids in a good school. It's got slow, steady growth, and not a whole lot of crime or anything. It's just a good place to raise a family."

With its heritage, Texas has to be one of the greatest states. It's the state where the current president is from. That means a whole lot. Texas gets a lot of recognition.

We get all kinds of people here—especially with it being a college town—we see people from all over the state. We

Bigger and better in Texas is the way I have always felt about it.

have kids from the larger towns and, of course, some from the smaller towns. There are so many different types and kinds of people. There are people from different countries that are here too. It's just a real good mix of the people who have come in. Everybody just seems to move in and stay. That's why I'm here in Nacogdoches. I moved to go to Stephen F. Austin University in '82—loved it and stayed here. Started raising a family and with the people that are here—nice atmosphere, no crime—it's one of the best places to live.

Family goes a long way; you want to carry that into the next generation. You can talk to just about anybody here in town and they can give you a story about something their family has done throughout the years here in East Texas and they want that to carry right on over to their kids. Most people tend to stay in the area even if they go away for a few years—they always come back and pass it along from one family member to the next.

It's just one of the great places and it's so convenient—we can go over into Louisiana if we ever want anything Cajun but you can always come back to Texas because everything's better in Texas. Bigger and better in Texas is the way I have always felt about it. There are some great states around us but I don't care to live anywhere but Texas. Speaking for myself, I don't care to live anywhere else but Nacogdoches. It's my hometown. It's one of the best places you'll ever live. It's convenient to the coast, Louisiana, even Oklahoma. We're in a nice place. There's no real crime. That's one of the main things I keep saying simply because I'm raising a family. With a 13-year old and a 10-year old, you want them in a good school system. You want them in a low crime area and you want a nice place like Nacogdoches to raise 'em. East Texas is the perfect place for us. I wouldn't consider living anywhere else.

BOB COLE

★ BIRTHPLACE ★
Hialeah, Florida

★ CURRENT RESIDENCE ★
Austin, TX

★ OCCUPATION ★
Radio Talk Show Host / Restaurateur

Bob Cole has been a morning radio fixture along with his broadcast partner,
Sammy Allred, for many years. They practice their craft on KVET-FM in Austin.
In addition to being one of the most recognizable radio personalities in town,
he is also the owner of two historic restaurants in Austin. He resurrected
both establishments from near ruin. Today Hills Cafe and The Tavern are
popular gathering places of people who appreciate "Old Austin". Keeping the
flavor and traditions of early Austin are one of Bob's continuing passions.

I 'm a preservationist of a self prescribed proportion. I'm attempting to stake my claim to preserve some of the great traditions of Austin, which have been restaurants, taverns, and live music venues.

When you stop and think about—and I have many times—people like to associate themselves with who they are and what they are. People associate themselves with things that represent how they want to be seen. Whether it's what they wear, what they drive, what radio station they listen to—it's why they proudly put stickers on their vehicles—they're saying—"This is who I am. I'm in this club. I'm of this class." The greater umbrella for all of that is where you live. Whether it's Abilene or Austin, Beeville or Dallas—Texans have that common bond of "We are proud." We are chauvinist about who we are and how big we are and how wonderful and braggadocio we are.

I remember in my first years in Texas, I heard a Texan admit that if you gave a Texan an enema, you could bury him in a shoebox. I thought long and hard about [not only] how true that was but how honest that was. It's the consummate example of how your attitude determines everything. Texans all have attitudes. Not necessarily bad ones. They have attitudes that help them cope—attitudes that evoke and emote pride. That's the common bond that I've seen in the people of Texas—that they love being here. So whether you're a 1960s hippie or a federal court judge—you have great pride in where you live. When that airplane lands from some convention you've been to in, say, Duluth, there's nothing better than home. As a guy who has lived in Miami and Washington, D.C., I found Austin and it became home. I was born and raised in Miami. It wasn't home then. Everybody was waiting to get out. Nobody that lived there was from there.

I understand what transitory communities are about. Even though you might end up leaving for a job opportunity, home's still in Texas. Home's always in

...if you gave a Texan an enema, you could bury him in a shoebox.

Texas. To quote Bum Phillips (and one of his successors, Jerry Glanville, who tried to adopt it but it didn't fly when he substituted the name of another state), "If you ain't sleepin' in Texas tonight, you're just campin' out."

We all define ourselves in some way, like what church we belong to. Texas is the great church. It's what we drive. It's an honesty. It's pride of association. There is nothing better than having a common bond with your fellow man. When we first begin a conversation when we meet somebody, whether it's a celebrity or a guy at the convenience store, we look for common ground. Whether it's the weather or "How ya feelin?" we're looking to establish commonality. At the end of the day, that's what all Texans have. There's pride in the fact that what we have in common is that we live in Texas.

Without hesitation, Austin is my favorite place. It just absolutely fine-tunes the whole concept of Texas. I lived in Houston before I lived in Austin. When I visited Austin that was my impression after twenty-four hours. This fine-tunes everything that's great about Texas (and brings it) into total focus.

My initial attraction to Austin was the people. I'm the kind of dude that it can ruin my day if somebody is rude to me in a store. It can absolutely ruin my day. It doesn't happen too much around here. The first time I saw Austin was in 1977, and I moved here within three weeks.

DON TAYLOR

★ BIRTHPLACE ★
Trenton, Missouri

★ CURRENT RESIDENCE ★
Canyon, TX

★ OCCUPATION ★
*Executive Director for incubator project at West Texas A&M University
and President and CEO of Data Star Communications*

*Although he is not a native Texan, this former national syndicated business columnist
turned his attention to economic development in the Panhandle. Taylor has lived in Canyon
since 1987. He first came to Texas in 1985 and lived for two years in Plainview,
which is between the south plains and the north plains in Hill County. This man was just
flat out smart and interesting. He can talk to you on just about any subject regarding Texas.
We met at the Ambassador Hotel restaurant in Amarillo, emptied the coffee pot,
and filled an entire morning with conversation.*

P lainview was the first place I ever lived where the storm windows would knock the velocity of the sand down low enough that it would fall out of the air and accumulate between the two windows. We've seen an inch of sand after a week of blow. Just add water and food and you could start your own ant farm. It'd be fun to watch.

I have two things that I do. One is that I work as the executive director of about a five million dollar project for West Texas A&M University that is building

You can drive down a highway where you've never been before in a car with out-of-state plates and you're going to get waved at by almost every native that's here.

seven business incubators in the Texas Panhandle—six in rural communities and one in Amarillo. I also own my own company, which is called Data Star Communications, and I'm president and CEO of that company and it is a company that provides business training and information to primarily U.S. Corporations, trade associations, and educational institutions.

I wrote a syndicated newspaper column for 13 years. I stopped writing at the end of 2001 so I'm recycling the column called "Minding Your Own Business." At one time it ran in 100 publications and circulated in all 50 states and 40 foreign countries. It ate eight hours a week out of my life and I decided at the end of 2001 I wanted those eight hours back. I no longer write.

The first book I wrote and co-authored with Jeannie Archer is called *Up Against the Wal-Marts*. The second book I wrote called *Solid Gold Success Strategies for your Business* was published in soft cover in 1996, *Wal-Mart* was published in 1994, and then I contributed to a third book recently, It's called *Confessions of Shameless Self-Promoters*.

I've traveled all 50 states, lived on the West Coast, Midwest, and various loca-

tions but we landed here by choice. In our careers we could live anywhere we wanted to and gave some thought to living in Hawaii but at this point we like Canyon, Texas. It is a comfortable, conservative place to live and since I was a Midwestern and fiscal conservative, I find it very easy to live in Canyon. People here, interestingly enough—if you were to change the seed corn caps—are typical of those you would find throughout the agriculture belt, particularly through the Midwest from Wyoming, Nebraska, Colorado, Kansas, Missouri, Illinois, Iowa, Ohio, even in Kentucky some of the ag production areas in the southeastern states. You will find those folks who are close to the land concerned about what's going on. They live mostly within their means and make do with what they got. They utilize the philosophy that I've kind of adopted as my own called "Use it up, wear it out, make do, do without." They're just good, workin', honest people of integrity. I find myself much more comfortable living in that kind of environment than in the suburbs of Chicago where the people are certainly fine or in southern California where everybody's got their own thing to do and their own axe to grind. I find it easier to live where neighbors are still neighbors.

You can drive down a highway where you've never been before, in a car with out-of-state plates, and you're going to get waved at by almost every native that's here. That's just something you do. You go down the road and you find yourself waving at that car that goes by. Maybe here in the Panhandle we have a lot of miles between communities and ranches and between houses. Out here, if you need me, just wave. I haven't analyzed or figured it out but people here really pitch in to help out. They really have the neighborly spirit.

Even with the distance, there's closeness there. They rally around their sports teams, their school systems, their communities, their fairs, and traditional events. That's not dissimilar to where I was raised or other parts of the country where people still have that—what I call—attitude of community. It can be that way even in a town the size of Amarillo. Amarillo, being 75,000 or 80,000 people, is an amazing community. People are proud to be from Amarillo, even though many of us are not native Texans. I think I was 39 years old when I came to Texas. I've been here 18 years and truly love it. There is not another place I'd rather live.

There is a state pride. Maybe it's the varied history. And maybe it's because Texas has some real identifiable heroes. The Alamo and the Battle of Adobe Wells took place right up here in the Texas panhandle. A few well-armed buffalo hunters held off the attacks of the Indians for several days, even though they were greatly outnumbered and low on provisions. But because they were buffalo hunters who knew how to fire their rifles and make their shots count, they were able to survive that raid. The Alamo is something every Texan takes pride in—that a few withstood many because they believed strongly in a cause. Texas has a great amount of history, a great amount of diversity, culturally and geographically. Almost everyone can find something about Texas to like and be proud of. But, certainly we have our warts.

If you take just the top 26 counties in the squared part of the Texas Panhandle, you will find seven states that would fit into that geographic area. Now that is just one little portion of Texas.

I'm not going to suggest that we secede, but interestingly enough we have a state representative still in the legislature who is very bright, very articulate, by the name of David Swinford. He represents Potter and Moore Counties—Potter being the northern part of Amarillo, Moore being the city of Dumas. He is from Dumas. He at one time, perhaps in jest, perhaps somewhat seriously, suggested that the top 26 counties of the Texas Panhandle should secede from the state of Texas because we are actually closer to several other state capitols than we are Austin. (Amarillo is closer to four other state capitols—Oklahoma City, Albuquerque, Denver, Topeka—than it is to its own capitol in Austin.) You can drive to any of those in fewer hours than you can go to Austin.

But he suggested that maybe this Panhandle area could secede and become a state because we are rich in many agricultural and oil & gas assets. We have a pretty good base. What we lack is population—we're about 400,000 population. Some people obviously thought Swinford had gone batty when he made that suggestion. There were others of us who said, "Ummm, that's not really such a bad idea." With Amarillo as the capitol, we could make a pretty good case for being a state.

We think of ourselves as Texans even if we're transplanted. There is some phenomena related to living in Texas. Someone once told me that if I wore out a pair of boots in the Panhandle, I would never leave. That's when I lived in Plainview. A couple of years later I moved 60 or 75 miles north, but I was still in the Panhandle. Texas is a wonderful place to live from a people standpoint.

I also personally believe that we have some of the greatest weather in the country. We have mild sunny winters. Yes, we have those three days a year when those "blue northers" come through and coincide with the highest tourism days. We do that intentionally, those people going across I-40 who get stranded in the blizzard will tell that story 11 million times over the next year, which keeps a lot of the riff-raff from coming to this area. I say that in jest, of course.

The Texas Panhandle is a great secret. We have beautiful falls. We have windy

We think of ourselves as Texans even if we're transplanted.

springs, but they're gorgeous. There is enough winter to keep the insect population down and kill some of the bad stuff. The summers are hot and dry. Hot is not a problem as long as there is minimal humidity. You go to other parts of the state, Austin included, certainly Dallas–Fort Worth, Houston, San Antonio, you get hot and wet. It's four times as miserable as being hot and dry. If you can find shade, you're gonna be okay.

I really believe that the state of Texas would never dissolve itself because people are proud that we have a Panhandle. People in South Texas and North Texas are proud that we have a Corpus Christi, a Houston, and a San Antonio. You've got El Paso with its western legend and the others— yeah it's twelve hours of nothin' between here and there but we're still proud of that nothin'. That's part of what makes us the largest state in the continental U.S.

Even in the fictional descriptions of Texas, most of those people come across as that clear eyed, hard workin', where their handshake is their word. Their word is good. They have integrity—even the scoundrels—even the bandits—even the gunman had a different code. You hear of the Code of the West. I think there was a Code of Texas. When Texans went out of this area to find jobs or they followed the cattle drives north and stalled, they still had that code of ethics that they stuck with. You know, I'd never mistreat a lady because I'm a Texan. Were there scoundrels who mistreated ladies? Certainly, but they probably came from somewhere else—at least in the minds of the Texans. They weren't real Texans.

Texas has the Western magic. It has the cowboy magic. It has the rodeo magic. That plays well in many European and many other foreign countries. The things fascinate the Europeans that we do like planting Cadillacs in a field or put a corrugated band of metal around the top of a plateau so under certain light condition that it appears that that plateau is floating above itself. The blue gray metal sort of looks like the sky and it appears that plateau just sits up there above itself. Not many places do that sort of thing. It's a real Texas character that did that named Stanley Marsh. Yeah, he's a character alright—not necessarily typical of what built Texas but certainly typical of second, third generation Texas wealth.

You know what's interesting? In casual conversation, I seldom have people tell me that they are a "native Texan." But if you probe a little or ask the question— "now, were you raised in Canadian or in Perryton? Has Dumas always been your home?"—they will not say, "Oh yes, I was raised in Dumas." They will say, "Oh yes, I'm a native Texan." I believe it's that Texas identity. Every little community and every big town belongs to the state of Texas. Perhaps that is something that is different than most other states. I'll have to tell you honestly, I don't notice the arrogance so much. These are calm and hard working people. They're too busy and in some cases too poor to be very arrogant. Are they proud of their heritage? Certainly. Are they proud to be in the Texas Panhandle? Absolutely. Do they enjoy the quality of life they are living? You bet, without a doubt.

Houston, TX

★ BIRTHPLACE ★
Houston, TX

★ CURRENT RESIDENCE ★
Houston, TX

★ OCCUPATION ★
Budding Writer

Vonceia exudes pride for both her state and her city.

The way one perceives Texas is directly related to one's experience with the state.

I think Texas is so special because the land is like the people... diverse and welcoming. Even after all this time, Texas is changing and growing. It's never stagnant.

To be a native Texan means that you are adaptable. It means that you understand how the rest of the world works, yet still retain a sense of what's important in life. It means that you can appreciate wide, open spaces as well as lonely seashores.

It means that you can see that there is really no conflict with modern technology and down home life.

Like the old saying goes, "There's no place like home." Houston is my town, my city. I've lived here all of my life and watched as it grew and changed. It's Space City. It's a microcosm of the world's population.

It's a business town with a great arts and culture community. At the same time, it's a town of history where every year, old and young are treated to a taste of yesterday through the Livestock Show and Rodeo. It's a city of tolerance and opportunity as well. Every culture who migrates to Houston has a chance to put down roots and thrive. It's a city where neighbors still care about neighbors and help is never more than a handshake away.

Texas derives its name from the word "Tejas"... pronounced, "Tay-haas." It is thought to refer to the remnants of various tribes...the Nasoni, Nabedache, Hainai and the Nacogdoche. The Handbook of Texas says the French and Spanish knew the Tejas as the Hasinai. The word itself is thought to be a Spanish pronunciation of the Hasinai word for friend. It is said these were the first words with which the natives greeted the first Europeans. The word has also been interpreted as meaning "ally."

JOE YURICK

★ BIRTHPLACE ★
Morristown, NJ

★ CURRENT RESIDENCE ★
Austin, TX

★ OCCUPATION ★
Operations Director Customer Service, SITEL Corp.

Joe is another transplant who you could not dynamite out of Texas.
He has completely assimilated into the lifestyle and he totally understands the
mindset. At one point, Joe and I worked together. When he became aware I was
writing a book about Texas, he took a real interest in the project. I already knew
of his strong feelings about Texas. As we talked it wasn't long before we agreed to meet
for a couple of cold ones in Luckenbach, Texas. It was through him I met
Sheriff Marge of Luckenbach. I found Joe's story of Texas not unlike many
transplants who have discovered Texas is the place to call home.

I came here right before Thanksgiving in 1977. I was young at the time and I was hitchhiking down to Florida to take care of my uncle's ranch and got as far as Houston, Texas. I called him to tell him that I was on my way and found out he didn't need anybody. So actually, I got stuck in Texas—in Houston—and I just ended up staying there for ten years.

I had never lived in a big city like Houston before—it really grew on me—just the atmosphere, the different climate, the different type of people, the sports in Houston. I had never been around any type of professional sports environment. The employment opportunities available at the time were tremendous. I just enjoyed it and decided to stay. I also met somebody over the first six months—probably my first girlfriend that I fell in love with. She was a born and bred Houstonian and the roots of her and her family were about 60 feet into the ground and she wasn't going anywhere.

Texas is so large and there are so many diverse areas within Texas, it's really a country of it's own. If you want to live in a high profile, fast moving city, you have Houston and Dallas. If you want to live in a younger, more musically oriented environment, there's Austin. And you also have the very laid back West Texas, East Texas or the Johnson Cities of the world. I have some property in Johnson City, so even though I live and work in a hustle and bustle environment, on the weekends I have the opportunity to be in a very laid back environment. You find any and every kind of ethnic background within the cities. Everybody seems to get along very well, for the most part. Do we still have things like racism and

> I really didn't think I'd be here 26 years but it would probably take a wrecking crew and a wrench to get me out of Texas now.

hatred? Absolutely, but you don't see it as much here—at least in Austin—as you would in some other cities.

That extra gene you talk about I would say is, in my mind, pride. They're very proud of their state and what it means to the rest of the nation. On the male side of that gene, I'd say that gene is the gentleman part of it. On the female side, it's the gentlewoman piece of it. They'll do anything and everything to make people aware of how important it is to live in Texas. Texans tend to help each other out. I've seen and been in it—in situations where tornadoes have hit, or floods, even hurricanes. It's amazing how quick families, friends and neighborhoods get together to help each other get back up on their feet. It happens naturally. You don't really see a whole lot of people picking up the phone asking for a lot of help. It's there and it's there as quickly as possible.

What's my favorite place in Texas? That's easy. Luckenbach. Of course, I'm a Willie Nelson fan. I've seen him live quite a few times. I went to Luckenbach back in '77. It's very laid back. I can go there on any given weekend and there will be two, three or four people playing the guitar, singing together, having a good time—never having done it before. You can actually hear the harmony within the first couple of songs.

That place for me is my—how do I want to put this—it's my Valium. I can go in there and I can be wound so tight that I feel like I'm going to lose it. Then I spend a few hours in Luckenbach playin' washers, talking to people that either have never been there before or locals—I knew Marge, the Sheriff, for many, many years. That's the place I can go and unwind and just get everything back together. I would also say Johnson City is probably my second favorite place.

I really didn't think I'd be here 26 years but it would probably take a wrecking crew and a wrench to get me out of Texas now. I love it. I will live and die here. I wasn't born here but I got here as fast as I could. You've heard that before but it's true. I enjoy it. It's a good place for anyone to be or raise a family.

During the ten years I spent in Houston—probably never a week went by when I didn't think about moving back to Oregon or Virginia where I got my education. If I had stayed in Houston, I probably would have ended up moving back somewhere closer to family but the girlfriend that I had—well, that didn't work out. I was on my own. I had the opportunity to move to Austin in '85 or '86; that's really when I decided to stay in Texas. I've been here since then. I love the city. There's so much to do here. I found Johnson City during that time. I met my wife after being here about a year. I didn't have a father growing up. Her family took me in as not only her boyfriend and eventually as her husband but also as a son. I like that. It's a family background. That's probably the biggest thing that has kept me here. The family bond is very tight. Not that I don't miss the snow and the skiing or the seasons. That's probably the biggest thing I miss. You don't really have the seasons like I grew up with—but I've gotten over it because I also enjoy snow on one day and 75 degrees the next.

BARBARA JENNISON

★ BIRTHPLACE ★
Tye (Taylor County), TX

★ CURRENT RESIDENCE ★
San Angelo, TX

★ OCCUPATION ★
Retired Jill-of-all-trades

*The eloquence of Ms. Jennison's words are simple and direct. You can almost feel
her passion as she captures several of the core elements that are Texas.*

Texas is so large that no matter what kind of landscape you like—we got it. I personally like South Padre Island and Lake of the Pines. These diverse landscapes appeal to my multi-faceted personality. Texas means, and is, friendly—even to Yankees!

What's it mean to be a native Texan? Bragging rights! After all, we have cowboys, beaches, gentlemen, gentility and friendliness.

My favorite place in Texas is South Padre Island. It appeals to the solitude I like. I spent one relaxing summer vacation there with my late husband and our four daughters.

What's it means to be a native Texan is bragging rights!

There is no truth to the rumor that the state tree is an oil derrick.
Nor is the state bird a construction crane.

The official state bird is the Mockingbird not the mosquito
as some along the Texas Gulf Coast might suggest.

The Armadillo is the official state mammal.

The first official rodeo was held on July 4th, 1883 in Pecos.

SHELLEY BUECHE

★ BIRTHPLACE ★
Houston, TX

★ CURRENT RESIDENCE ★
Austin, TX

In her e-mail, Shelley talks about different parts of Texas.
One thing is certain: if you live somewhere in Texas for awhile and decide
you want to move to a totally different location, and still stay in Texas,
just drive about 200 miles in any direction and settle down.
You can live in a completely different world and you won't need new license plates.

I have been in Austin since 1960. I am a native Texan. Texas has it all—rambling rivers, mountains, lakes, cosmopolitan cities and towns with a population of two (isn't that Luckenbach?). My favorite place in Texas is the Hill Country. I love traveling the road from Kerrville through Ingram to Hunt, the road that winds along the river. Kerrville to me is the perfect size, but I've heard that the citizens of Kerrville and Fredericksburg are complaining about "all these big city slickers" moving in and ruining their town.

In Texas, you can find people from every ethnic group and every country in the world. I've never been to Crawford, but I would love to check out President Bush's ranch.

JAMES FERGUSON

★ BIRTHPLACE ★
Port Arthur, TX

★ CURRENT RESIDENCE ★
Pflugerville, TX

★ OCCUPATION ★
Accountant

James, I call him, "Ferg," is an old college friend.
He dropped this entry through my web site at www.TweedScott.com.
We met when we were both business majors at Lamar University back in the early 1970s.
We still believe we were the very first people to come up with the idea of inline roller skates.
We just never did anything about it. He's a bright and sensitive guy and I have
always known of his deeply rooted love of Texas.

From the day you are born a Texan, you hear stories of Stephen F. and Davy Crockett. We believe that Texas is special and we are special because we get to live in such a great place. Texas truly is a state of mind. We are better because we get to live in this great state. By the Grace of God, I was born Texan and those few unlucky, intelligent folks who were not as lucky...got here as fast as they could.

I was born in Southeast Texas, lived in Houston for a while, East Texas for a while and now in the Texas Hill Country. It seems that no matter where I live in Texas, it is still God's country and nothing else compares.

Texas is the only state whose flag can fly
at the same height as the United States flag, "Old Glory."

The land area of Texas is larger than all of New England,
New York, Pennsylvania, Ohio and Illinois combined.

The defenders of the Alamo came from 22 states and 6 countries.

El Paso is 27 miles closer to San Diego than it is to Houston.

The original name of Austin was Waterloo.

STEVE FALLON

★ BIRTHPLACE ★
San Antonio, TX

★ CURRENT RESIDENCE ★
Robinson, TX (a suburb of Waco)

★ OCCUPATION ★
Executive Director, Texas Sports Hall of Fame

T exas is special because it can be so many things to so many people. Also, people tend to look at you with a bit of envy when you say you are from Texas. We are a state with a lot of backbone and sex appeal!

My hometown of Waco has a little bit of everything. It can be "big city" with its modern conveniences. It can be "country" because there are so many places where there is solitude and anonymity. It is one of the state's best kept secrets.

Being a native means never having to say you're sorry. State pride like this is not found in every state.

ROBERT HIGGINBOTHAM

★ BIRTHPLACE ★
Beaumont, TX

★ CURRENT RESIDENCE ★
Canyon, TX

★ OCCUPATION ★
HVAC Technician
Canyon Independent School District

Several times over the years I have heard Texans say that they could
always tell the moment they crossed into Texas. Sometimes it's the texture
of the road, and some say they can tell the difference in the air. I have run into
such a person in Canyon, Texas, just south of Amarillo. This turns out to be
a common occurrence. Maybe Robert, like others, is just psychic.

There is a certain feeling I get anytime I come back to Texas. It just feels like no matter what state line or border I cross whenever I come back into Texas I feel at home. It is just a certain feeling inside I get that tells me I am home. I get to kick back and relax and be me. When I am in other states, I always wonder, "Are they going to be friendly because I am a Texan, are they going to belligerent because I am a Texan?" "Do they like or dislike Texans?" Some people are ecstatic to be in the presence of a Texan and other people want to try to knock you down because you are a Texan. Every time I have gone out of the state, you might say out of my country, I have always felt like I am not at home. I can't kick back and relax. When I get in the state of Texas I can because I know I am amongst friends no matter where I am.

Texas has an image everywhere. When I was in Thailand one of the Thais would ask a guy where he was from. One would say, "I'm from Tennessee," "I'm from Washington," "I'm from California," "I am from Maine," or whatever. They would smile politely and say, "Hi." But you say you're from Texas and they would perk up and say, "Oh, from Texas!—Oil wells, cowboys, Indians." Texas, Tejas, means friendly. Perhaps subliminally we are trying to live up to the name of our state—friendly. We are trying to be friendly people.

My favorite place in Texas is the panhandle. There's something about it being so flat. Sometimes in the morning, you look out there and you see that sun rising and maybe there's a thunderhead over there in the distance with the sun hittin' the clouds in such a way that it gives you a brilliant sunrise or sunset—and there's nothing to block the view. There's a vast openness where at night you can get away from town, look up and see stars forever and ever. Or look out and you can tell where the communities are nearby from the glow of their lights. You can see forever.

> When I get in the state of Texas I can relax because I know I am amongst friends no matter where I am.

A friend of mine took some pictures of thunderheads building in the distance. One picture just happened to have an old windmill in the front. Here's that old windmill sitting there and this huge thunderhead just building and building. He wanted to paint a picture of that but he never got to finish it. It took three or four pictures to encompass that one shot. The vastness of it all is amazing. Back in the early days when cows were being branded, there was not a tree in sight—and not even a fence most of the time. It was the days of the open range. You're able to breathe in Texas.

Just like the song says, on a clear day you can see forever. It's just about that way. It's clean air too because there's not much up here to pollute it. Just being in Texas, there is something about the air. I swear it even changes in an airplane. Coming back from Thailand, I was between Albuquerque and Lubbock. The pilot hadn't said anything about fastening seatbelts or we're getting ready to land in Lubbock. Somewhere in flight, I felt a change in the air. I knew I was home. I could just feel when I crossed that state line. 'Cause it seemed like there was a change in the air even though we were supposed to breathing the same air as New Mexico. There's something about when you cross that line—you feel it. My son, Kevin and I went to a basketball game in New Mexico. Going over, we felt a change in the air on the Texas-New Mexico the state line. Coming back, we felt that same change only the opposite way. If you're a Texan, you know it. You know you're home when you're in Texas. No matter where it is in the state.

The Buick Electra was named after Electra Waggoner Biggs. Her brother-in-law was Harlow H. 'Red' Curtice, the President of Buick Motors of General Motors. In 1959 he named one of his luxurious Buick models, Electra. She was also a nationally known sculptor. Perhaps her best known work was of an American icon, Will Rogers upon his horse, "Soapsuds". She was commissioned to create the work after Rogers was killed in a plane crash in Alaska in 1935. She passed away in 2001.

TIM McCLURE

★ BIRTHPLACE ★
Corsicana, TX

★ CURRENT RESIDENCE ★
Austin, TX

★ OCCUPATION ★
Advertising Executive, A Founder of GSD&M

*The IMAX movie format is awe-inspiring. We are fortunate enough to have an
IMAX theatre at the Bob Bullock Museum in Austin. They show a movie several times
every day called* Texas the Big Picture. *I sat there mesmerized as I watched it.
It covered everything I have ever felt about Texas. Tim McClure was the man behind
the movie. Before we sat down to do the interview in his office at GSD&M, one of the
biggest and most respected advertising agencies in the world, I told him how big a fan I was
of the movie. I have actually paid to see it seven or eight times, always bringing
several people along with me. If you come to Austin to see me, we'll go to the museum
and watch it together. I told Tim that I just loved the movie and told him that I could have
written that script. Talk about sticking your boot in your mouth, I didn't realize that
he wrote the script! He completely captured the essence of Texas.
He touched on several aspects of the Texas way during our time together.*

I f you ask anybody from any other place on the planet where they're from they will generally say, "I'm from New York City, I am from Tokyo," or, "I am from Duluth, Minnesota." A Texan will always say, "I'm from Texas." They won't tell you the town or city they're from—they say, "I'm from Texas." So there is an incredible sense of pride about being from Texas that I doubt exists in Rhode Island for instance. What makes us feel that way is a much larger question. We could spend hours on that. I just made a movie on Texas (*Texas the Big Picture*). So my answer to that is Texas is not just a state of mind. It's a state of heart and a state of soul. I think it involves all three of those things in a semi-religious experience that you encounter when you're born here and grow up here. One that other people experience only as soon as they can get here.

There are two things that distinguish people that don't really fit in. Either you say, "You're not from around here," or you say, "That boy's just not right." So I wouldn't say that my wife's not right but I would say she's not from around here. She was an oil brat and lived all over the world. So when I coerced her down to Texas to marry me, the first thing I did was drive her down to San Antonio, show her the Alamo and take her across the street to the IMAX movie there on the Alamo. We came out of it and I said, "So?" She said, "Okay, I get it.'

I said good, "You know what it's like to be a Texan."

She said, "I have no idea what it's like to be a Texan but I get it now—why you people are the way you are." She went on to explain that she had never heard of the Alamo in her life—nor did she think anybody north of the Red River had heard of the Alamo.

This thing we had considered to be the national if not international interplanetary shrine to freedom was sort of a Texas thing. So I think Texans internalize things about Texas and they sometimes may make the assumption the whole world knows about it. Not the clichés of cowboys and tumbleweeds but the things that make Texas unique. That's a long list.

When I was asked to be on the Foundation Board of the Bob Bullock Texas State History Museum, I said, "I would be happy to serve in the board on one condition—that you not call it the Texas State History Museum."

So I think Texans internalize things about Texas and they sometimes may make the assumption the whole world knows about it.

They asked, "Why?"

And I said, "Do you know how many museums have the word 'Texas' in their names just in Austin, Texas, not to mention throughout the state?"

It was a pretty big number. They said they had to call it that by state charter. So I asked if I could give a nickname for it—"The Story of Texas." When you drive by the Bullock Museum, if you look above the part that says the Texas State History Museum, it says "The Story of Texas".

I am convinced that the stories of Texas have always been told around campfires. I suspect that thing you call the "T Chromosome" may be the result of the hundreds of years of stories told around campfires—the legends and myths and mysteries that have been passed along. It's a rough and tumble place. I think people have grown to love the state for its rugged beauty, its friendliness, and its sense of character and honor.

—❊—

There is a struggle with anything good that ever happens. Consider that they built the city of Houston in the middle of a bayou. I think the people coming across from Mexico into West Texas— the Badlands as they are often called— had to have seen something that you or I might not see otherwise. They thought the reward was worth the risk and the effort. I think struggle and opportunity are the things that bind us together. We were once a nation and perhaps Texas, more than any other state, is as much a

melting pot as the whole United States. There is basically every race, color and creed represented here—and all very strongly. One of the first French Legations in the country was in Austin Texas. So the French, the Germans, the Poles, the Mexicans, and the Texicans— as they became known—were all a part of it. My family's ancestors were from Philadelphia. I had a great grand-father who was at the Alamo. He was a McClure, he was Irish and he was smart enough to leave before the battle. But he was in the Texas Revolutionary Army, stationed there and moved through the area on the way to somewhere else before the battle. He did lose an eye in a later battle.

—❊—

Sunday Houses were small houses on the outskirts of a city or town like Austin, which back then was called Waterloo, where people would come and stay when they'd go into the city for Sunday services and so forth. They could go to that house and spend the night before going back to where they lived in outlying areas. I always thought that was great to get to church services from great distances. I guess that's what we call guesthouses now.

—❊—

There are a couple of things that my partners and I—who founded this advertising agency straight out of the University of Texas back in 1971—have been involved in and that we're very proud of relating to Texas. One of which is the campaign that I wrote back in 1985, *Don't Mess With Texas* which went on to become the most successful anti-litter campaign in history. We reduced litter on our state's highways by 72 percent, which was an amazing story and one of the best campaigns we've ever done. We also created the campaign for state tourism, which you'll recognize: *Texas. It's Like A Whole Other Country.* That kind of gets at your T-Chromosome.

I think that it is like a whole other country. Generally, in the marketing business you try to compare yourself to somebody. We found that when we competed with other states we were sort of on the low end of the totem pole. When you ask people where they would like to travel on vacation they would say California, New York or Florida. Texas was way down the list. So we decided rather than try to move up the list for a great deal of money and time it would take us, we would position ourselves as a whole other country and show the similarities of the state to all parts of this country and other countries. Almost overnight, in marketing terms, we became the second most qualified destination for travel by suggesting there was a lot more variety here than anyone ever imagined. We would show them things like the river in San Antonio. On the screen it would say "This is not the French Riviera" and we'd show the beaches.

We have one of the longest coastlines in America. So we're very proud of that campaign.

Texas was once its own country. It is a country that has such a diverse influx of people from around the world and a lot of those traditions have guided what Texas is about. It's hard to qualify Texas or Texans. You can't say they are mostly Germanic or French or mostly Mexican. They are not mostly anything. They're mostly Texan, born out of that melting pot of cultures that made it what it is.

> When you said you were from Texas, even though there would be some rolled eyes, at least it meant something.

The other thing that amazes me is the geology and geography of the state of Texas. There are myths we had to dispel when people thought that we were basically a desert with tumbleweeds and cowboys. You find out there are mountains, Piney Woods, great plains and coastlines and things that you don't normally imagine are in Texas, simply because the place is so darned big geographically. I'm sure you've heard this before, but it is geographically true that when you leave Austin and arrive in El Paso, which is still in Texas, you are half way to Los Angeles.

Oddly enough, when I was eleven years old, I got on a train in Dallas, and took that train to Boulder, Colorado for the Boy Scout Jamboree. I got to see President Eisenhower in an open

Cadillac driving through the Boy Scout camp. And I realized how homesick I was for Texas and how impressive it was to other people.

When you said you were from Texas, even though there would be some rolled eyes, at least it meant something. You find that not only in this country but in places like England and Australia. When I was in Australia, they asked me, "Where are you from?" I'd say I'm from Texas and they'd want to know what Texans thought of Australians.

—◄◄═══►►—

Well, you either are or not a native Texan. We are fond of saying you may not be from Texas but you got here as quick as you could. It is probably the greatest source of pride, I think, to say you were born in Texas. I think being born in Texas gives you a unique perspective. Most Texans, at least when I was growing up, didn't venture very far out of Texas. Until I was 18 years of age, I only left Texas one time and that was for a Boy Scout Jamboree in Colorado. There was no point to go anywhere else because any direction you pointed yourself and went, you were still in Texas. So I didn't do a lot of traveling. I've done a tremendous amount of traveling since then. I just got back from

Antarctica so I've seen the rest of the world but I would still rather come back to Texas than any other place on the planet. I add, parenthetically, come back to *Austin*, Texas.

Austin is a true oasis in the middle of the state and to me it is a social, mental, and spiritual oasis. The fact that it is so beautiful, covered in trees leading into the Hill Country, it is a liberal interpretation of the rougher edges of Texas. It's a very young city. I think the average age in Austin, some years ago, was only about 22 or 23 so it is very young and very progressive. When I was in school here back in the late '60s and early '70s, we were sort of the Berkeley of Texas. I think there is a liberal point of view that is very refreshing. It's a "young at heart" part of Texas. It's not as dyed in the wool as perhaps some other parts of Texas, where if you're not from around here, you're considered an outsider. Austin is very welcoming. It's a wonderful place.

I got the absolute honor, at this point in my career and my life as a Texan, to write a love letter to my state in the form of an IMAX movie. I got say thank you. That will always be indelibly etched in my soul that I got to say thank you to the state that has meant so much to me.

—◄◄═══►►—

Artwork: Jamie Rood

Austin, Texas

Austin artist Jamie Rood works in both two and three dimensional mediums. See this stylized Austin skyline in full color at www.JamieRood.com.

IT'S ALL ABOUT the PRIDE

Texas is the only state to have the flags of six nations fly over it.
They are Spain, France, Mexico, Republic of Texas,
Confederate States of America and the United States.

Showing Texas Pride

While every state exhibits its own regional pride, as they should, Texans are unique in the ways they displays their pride. Where else can one find items ranging from frying pans and ice cube trays to tortilla chips shaped like their state? If it can be marketed or sold, there is a good possibility you'll find it in the shape of Texas. I've seen no other place in the country where the state's colors and symbols are so commonly and prominently displayed.

Rare is the Texas community where the Texas Flag is not visibly flown. Neighborhood after neighborhood, you only have to drive past a few houses or blocks before you come across the lone star displayed. It is not uncommon to find people who have a flagpole or two installed on their property flying the Texas flag right along side "Old Glory." If only one flag is unfurled, often, it's the Texas colors displayed.

Texas lends itself to marketing. Think about it. Here's a state so big that a number of automobile manufacturers have designed Texas models or packages directly targeted at Texas' consumers. Ford has developed a King Ranch model of pickup truck. I don't believe I've seen the Wisconsin version of the Chevy Trailblazer.

As you will see in the following pictures, the Texas colors and symbols are displayed frequently and in almost limitless imaginative ways. Perhaps one reason for this is that the colors and symbols naturally lend themselves to be used in a number of ways. The Texas state colors are essentially the same as the national colors. Americans are proud of their homeland and are quick to wrap themselves in the red, white, and blue when the mood or the situation arises. Texans are no less proud of their "country" and embrace all the symbolism that is part of being a Texan—and Texas has plenty to choose from. Make no mistake, there is a nationalism that thrives in Texas, and they love to show it. It was pointed out recently that Texans never refer to their boundaries as state lines—they are called borders. I suspect that is a throwback to the days of the Republic of Texas—after all, sovereign nations have borders.

There are infinite ways to market Texas. Why, they even have a "National

Beer of Texas!" You'd be hard pressed to name another state that has a "national beer!"

The most prominent displays include the outline of Texas, the state flag, the Alamo profile, lone stars, longhorns, cowboys, boots— even the capitol building in Austin features elaborate door hinges. Regardless which corner of the state you encounter as you travel across Texas, you are always reminded that you are deep in the heart of Texas.

JIM GREGORY

★ BIRTHPLACE ★
Brady, TX

★ CURRENT RESIDENCE ★
Austin, TX

★ OCCUPATION ★
Co-Owner, Texas Disposal Systems

*This interview came as an outcropping of a magazine story I was assigned to do
for* Country Line Magazine *in Austin. Jim and his brother operate Texas Disposal Systems.
It is a large landfill operation, perhaps one of the best run in the nation.
On a large portion of the property, which is not being used for the landfill operation,
they have an exotic game ranch. There is everything there from American bison to zebras.
There's Ostriches, wildebeest and any number of herds of deer and antelope.
While interviewing him for the magazine story, I could sense his strong feelings
over being a Texan and decided that he needed to be a part of this effort.*

I was born in Brady, which is the "Heart of Texas." They got that back in the 1940s, probably because it was the closest community to the geographical center of Texas.

My wife is from California and we go back and forth so we do get to travel a lot. I've traveled around the world. We hunt Africa and we do different things like that. When people find out you're from Texas, it's almost a special thing. My son went on a mission trip for six months in Europe and Bosnia. His name was "Texas." It's like you're from the United States and you're from Texas. There is an arrogance to being from Texas.

I've had some occasions when dealing with people from up north and they've looked at Texans as, I think, just a bunch of arrogant, dad-gum redneck cowboys that haven't got sense to get out of the rain. And we kind of enjoy that. We kind of say yeah, we are a little redneck. Yup, we drink a cold beer every night and, by God, my wife's fat and ugly but you know what? She's a dad-gum good cook and I love her, so you leave her alone. Does that make sense?

If you go anywhere in the world and tell people you're from Texas, you hear an amazement. Texas! Maybe it's from all those years of the Dallas Cowboys and the Tom Landry days when we were all about football. They out sold all the other football teams combined for years.

I don't think the difference is size because if you went by size, you know Alaska, by size, is larger. Maybe part of it is that arrogant attitude that appears to come across—and me being a Texan, I don't think it's arrogance. I think it's life. I think we are a little better down here. I think we do treat people better. Around here when you drive down the road, if I see you, I'm going to wave to

A real Texan knows and does the right thing.

you. Maybe not so much nowadays but back 25 years ago, if your pickup broke down on the road, you wouldn't sit there five minutes—somebody would pull up and say, "Hey man, whatsa matter? You got a problem?" Now things can be so dangerous that you don't see as much of that anymore. Still today, if your wife and kids were going over to Fredericksburg to go shopping and they break down in Johnson City out on the highway, it'd only be a few minutes before somebody is going to stop and help them. And I want to tell you that I'm proud of that. That's the "what goes around comes around" mentality. It's still like that in West Texas.

I go to San Angelo about once a month. I tell people out there that 25 years ago people did not use contracts when they made agreements. They shook hands. I want to tell you—that was binding.

A real Texan knows and does the right thing. That's what I like to think of as Texans. When you hear of Texans who were just out for the almighty dollar—that grieves me. These are Texans? There's always a bad apple in the bunch. The statement that your wife made at the supper table one night—that your son had something you would never have, that he was born in Texas—that is Texas. I'm sure she didn't mean it in an arrogant way. She meant it in a proud way.

I really truly am proud to say I'm from Texas. When we were in New York people would say, "Aww, you're from Texas." You know what? I don't hang my head at all. I say, "I dad-gum sure am. You ever been down there? You oughta come down there some time."

I don't know if being a native Texan is something you can tell people what it's like. I don't mean this in a bad way, but that is something you, as a non-native, will never be able to experience—your son will. He already does.

The U.S. Army received a shipment of 32 camels in an effort
to utilize them as pack animals in the hostile desert environment
of West Texas and beyond. The experiment was an abysmal failure.
Rumors still persist of sightings of camels in the western deserts.
As far as anyone can tell, the sightings are just that—rumors.

DAVID LACY

★ BIRTHPLACE ★
Dallas, TX

★ CURRENT RESIDENCE ★
Dallas, TX

We ran into David Lacy at the Texas State Fair just a few steps from the Cotton Bowl.

This conversation touched on several ideas on how

people in Texas relate to their state.

What makes Texas special is Texas people. Born and raised in Texas. The free spirit. Helping other people out. Texas is so big. You've got so many different cultures here. And we're all Texas proud. I was born in Dallas, raised in Mesquite, moved away from here out to East Texas for about ten years and I came back to the Dallas area. In every part of Texas there is a good ol' home feeling. You go away and when you come back people treat you just as nice as they can be. It's just like you've been there your whole life. It is unique. I think it's due to the upraising of the people. From our forefathers all

The mentality of the people here in Texas and the mentality of people up north never ceases to amaze me how different they are.

the way up, it's just a set of values that have been handed down generation after generation.

Now, I have not been to every part of Texas. I have been to West Texas, North Texas, East Texas to the other side of Lufkin. I personally like Southeast Texas, all the pine trees. It's beautiful country. In West Texas, you've got hills. Some call them mountains. I've taken several courses of storm spotting because of when I was in East Texas. I'm a member of the police department over there and fire department. During storms we were trained to watch out for tornadoes and how to spot them. I spent a few weeks out in West Texas. You can see those thunderstorms miles away. In East Texas you've got all those pine trees—you're lucky if you find a good clear spot for twenty miles. In East Texas, I've seen several tornadoes touch down.

The biggest problem Texas has right now and the biggest fight that has been

> In every part of Texas there is a good ol' home feeling.

going on for, I'd say, a thousand years or more, is water rights. Every landowner has the right to water. You have a lot of people who want that right. That fight is going on all over the state—even Dallas. You wouldn't think Dallas would have that problem but Dallas does. Dallas does not have an endless supply of water. They're trying to build a lake up north from here to help service Dallas. A lot of people are trying to fight that. Their reason is they don't want to give up their land for this lake so that citizens here in Dallas will have drinkin' water.

We still have some of the oldest laws known to man on the books here. There is a law still in force today that if you're riding a horse, you're not allowed to carry a pair of wire cutters with you. It goes back to when people were putting up fences. The cattle men would be runnin' cows while the guys riding up ahead would just cut the fence to let the cows through. So they made that a law and as of today, it's still on the books.

JAMES M. WHITE

★ BIRTHPLACE ★
Austin, TX

★ CURRENT RESIDENCE ★
Austin, TX

★ OCCUPATION ★
Owner / Operator, The Broken Spoke

James is an Austin icon and owns, in my opinion, the quintessential Texas honky-tonk,
The Broken Spoke. If you want to spend a night listening to country music
in a genuinely Texan atmosphere, "The Spoke" is the place to be.
The people who have played here reads like the who's who of country and
western swing music. Although I have known him since the early 1980s,
it was not until we sat down for this conversation that I learned of the colorful
Texas Ranger background of his family. His Texan roots are well established.

The big thing about Texans is their pride. We've got something to be proud of. We have always been proud that we were once a nation. That's why we stand up and say, "We're from Texas because we fought to get our Texas independence." And later we joined the United States of America. That's what's been passed down in my family—we're proud of being Texans. We've done something no other state has done. We have something to be proud of not only because of what we did—like Ernest Tubb wrote a song that said, "There's a little bit of everything in Texas." There is a little of everything to do in Texas. The main thing is the friendly people. Wherever you go, people are more friendly when you come out and tell 'em you're from Texas. They've heard of Texas.

I went to England. They may not have heard of Idaho but they darn sure heard of Texas. The people are friendly people. It's just a feeling of pride. We probably brag more about our state than any other state in the Union because we do have something to brag about.

I'm proud of what my ancestors did. They fought for the Texas independence. They came here in 1836. There are Texas Rangers in my family. They settled the land and pioneered the land. There is something about the land in Texas. If you're fortunate enough to own a piece of ground here

in Texas, you can always reach down and grab yourself a handful of good Texas dirt—that alone makes you feel proud to be here.

I have people come up to me and talk about the Broken Spoke and say, "You've got a gold mine." I tell 'em it's kind of hard to dig and scratch through the dirt to find the gold. There's a lot of work involved. When I went in business here, a lot of people said, "You don't know what you're doing. You won't be here six months." Five years later the same people came by and said, "You had everything going for you."

Texans like to kid too. They can kid about themselves. It's good people that live here. Fortunately for us, a lot of people who come to Texas—we just want them to feel good about being here but we don't want to come down here and try and change anything either.

We probably brag more about our state than any other state in the Union because we do have something to brag about.

I think a lot of Texas has to do with the roots of it. They have a whole lot of people who come from all over the world who moved to—say, New York City. They don't know each other up there. When I was growing up in Austin, if I didn't know you, I knew one of your friends or I knew one of your relatives. It means a lot to grow up in a place where you have family values. You know the difference between right and wrong. Texans will fight for being right or wrong. That means a lot to us too. Something you don't want to dodge if you're in the right. Like an old Texas Ranger saying, "Nothin' stops a man in the right when he keeps on a comin'." I believe that a lot. I'm proud of my ancestors that were Texas Rangers. I think it is something to be proud of.

My great-great grandfather was James Madison Patton. He came to Texas in 1836 along with his father, Samuel Boyd Patton—they came from Alabama & Mississippi. The rest of my relatives came from Tennessee. They settled in the Austin area. My great-great grandfather was in the last Indian fight about a mile and half from the Broken Spoke over on Barton Creek. Him and a group of Texas Rangers at the time were camped out in 1846, where the capitol stands today. That was where the Ranger's headquarters was and they forded the Colorado River and captured a bunch of Indians. The first one jumped up and gave a war whoop—I think that was the Chief—and they shot him dead and the fight was on. When the Indians finally broke off the fight, one of them fired over his shoulder while he was leaving and hit one of the Rangers in the teeth. He died.

The family finally moved off the frontier to Oak Hill in 1870 and opened up a general store that has been in my family since 1879. Right now it's leased out to the Austin Pizza Garden. Years ago I ran a restaurant there called The Fortress. We're the ones who got the historical marker in 1970. Since then I did a lot of genealogy on my family. I'm a past president of Oak Hill Pioneer and of the Sons of the Republic of Texas. They meet out here at the Broken Spoke one Tuesday out of every month.

I've heard about the Texas Rangers all my life just like I've heard about Bob Wills all my life. I was fortunate to book some of my heroes at the Broken Spoke—like Bob Wills, Tex Ritter and Ernest Tubb, Roy Acuff. I'm a sixth generation Texan. Later I booked the Red Headed Stranger, Willie Nelson, when he had a song called "Mr. Record Man," that was the name of his band— Willie Nelson and the Record Men. I first booked him in 1967. I still get him out here today—I could book him for $800 a night years ago. I'm real proud of that.

I love the land. I love the Texas Hill country. When I grew up here, Austin was a sleepy little city. I still love Austin but I'm like everyone else—I don't like the traffic and the taxes that go along with it.

Folks ask, "Where's your gun?" or "Where's your horse?" I still kind of live that dream. I have horses and cattle and I've got plenty of guns. It's history that is always being instilled in people's minds. Wherever you go you ought to be glad you're from Austin, Texas. Deep in the heart of Texas—when I write a song or sing a song, it always makes me feel good when I say, "Deep in the heart of Texas."

The Broken Spoke was voted the Best Honky Tonk in Texas in 1990 by *Texas Highways*. *Entertainment Magazine* vot-ed us The Best Dancehall in Texas. *National Geographic* called us their favorite nightspot in Austin. The *[Austin] American Statesman* voted us the best Chicken Fried steak in Town. These accomplishments make it possible to keep things going. I like the people, they've been real good to me, I like to talk to them. They let me run the Broken Spoke—I get to live my dream.

I picked the name Broken Spoke because I wanted something "Texas." I wanted something Western. I was thinking about wagon wheels at the time. It came to me about this one old movie called *Broken Arrow* and so I said, "When I get out of the service I'll just get me a couple ol' wagon wheels and knock the spokes outta them and I'll name it the Broken Spoke." I figured that was all there was to it. I found out later there was a lot more to it than that. But I figure it was a good start anyway. This place has good heart and soul. If the walls could talk, what tales they could tell.

TERRY BOOTHE

★ BIRTHPLACE ★
Austin, TX

★ CURRENT RESIDENCE ★
Bee Cave, TX

★ OCCUPATION ★
Empresario

This man is one of my heroes. His passion is so deeply a part of him that you can feel it the moment you meet him. A part of his life's mission is to preserve the traditions and customs of Texas. The land has always been a part of his life. Owning your own piece of Texas is something tangible and worth possessing.

Terry Boothe has an unquestionable, passionate, devotion to Texas. Each year around Texas Independence Day, he throws a large party for his friends to preserve the traditions, ideals and values of Texas. As the twilight approaches, he invites several friends to read speeches, such as, Travis' letter from the Alamo. Still others perform songs written to honor Texas. He also gives awards recognizing individuals for their devotion to Texas. Then he stands up and gives a speech that exudes pride, attitude and a consummate love for the Lone Star State. The ceremonies close with canon salutes conducted by Texas Revolution Era re-enactors and the Texas A&M Aggie Corps of Cadets. It is both moving and exhilarating. It makes you, by God, proud to be a Texan. We begin with a short speech he delivered at one Texas Independence Day celebration...

"Today marks the anniversary of Texas sovereignty. I consider affiliation with the United States as incidental—just a convenience. The history of Texas along with the myth and legend are known worldwide. Why? Because the ideals that pioneer Texas stood for symbolized the best of the human spirit. Honor, dignity, self-reliance, and respect for the land—essential to sustain life. In spite of overwhelming odds these individuals, Anglo and Mexican alike, were willing to fight and die to preserve this against an oppressive government. Are the legends and myths of Texas history true and accurate? Well, I don't know. But I'll tell you this, if not, then they should have been. Because these stories symbolize the character that we should all strive for today. For without ideals what guides us? So today I tip my hat to Texas and the men and women who came before us, who in their own way have tried to manifest in their own lives the spirit of Texas."

⇥ ⇥

I suppose it starts with the geography. It starts with the land. It starts with the diversity of types of land all within one boundary that's identified as Texas. It ranges from the ocean to the deserts to the brush and cattle country to rolling plains to piney woods to rich agricultural property—to my knowledge unmatched in these fifty United States. Some may certainly have some exquisitely more beautiful scenery, but none quite as diverse. The geography, the dirt itself—what we call Texas is the respect, appreciation, and regard for that dirt by those who reside on it.

I don't know that it's exclusive to Texas. Most people like the geography and the dirt they grew up on because it's home. But I've never seen such a fierce loyalty—a feeling of being indigenous with the soils and with the particular piece of land and dirt as I have in Texas. Perhaps this is more universal than I think it is. The people and the land, certainly those several generations deep in it, it's a part of them and they are a part of it.

I suppose it's rooted in the history. The people who came here were trying to start over, not unlike the European settlers in one respect. But a second-generation settler—a generation removed from those that came over here—they were already over here. It was a starting over point and a dedication to that starting over with this particular piece of land.

I'm not an authority on Texas history although I'm quite familiar with a lot of different stories. But certainly, the early settlers faced a very hostile environment both from the Native Americans as well as from the extreme temperatures, the wilderness—the environment itself.

Let me make a point here. It's not that the Texas experience is unique. Certainly, the settlers who came to all parts of the West—or even the early settlers in the East—they all fought Indians and were dealing with extreme elements, but it was at a unique place in time in a very unique part of the world. There seemed to be a bond that developed. Look at the fierceness at which the Texas Rangers defended this country and tried to cope, and contain, and maintain the legitimate environment within which to live. The dedication is

incredible when you look back at the historical events.

---- ≡◆≡ ----

Texas was once its own country. The reality of establishing and developing one's own nation is a source of pride, a source of uniqueness which is very unique—which is something to brag about, which is something to hang your hat on. Consider the size of the state. Certainly until Alaska was annexed in 1959, Texas was the biggest. You had more braggin' rights. See when you tie that to the commitment those early settlers made and their progeny and all those people who have followed—you've got automatic braggin' rights. So this just exacerbates the attitude that one might develop.

I guess the crux of being a native Texan is Darrell Royal's old line, "Dance with those that brung ya." I always respected and appreciated people who were authentic. These were people who were a manifestation of their roots and of who they really were. I think the psychology books will tell us that we are indeed, down to our DNA, a part of our ancestors. We often do things that are involuntary. It's just a part of who we are. So to me, I had no choice. My family has been here since the 1840s. I'm sixth generation Texan.

When you can treasure your lineage, and you can trace back six generations in a region or an area that already has distinguished itself as something important in the annals in North American history, you feel it, it's real.

If I could have one wish, it would be that our traditional Texas culture would remain alive in our ever-changing contemporary society.

That's who I am. To deny that would have been foolish and artificial. I like all of the myths and the legends that Texas represents. I, in fact, feel like I've manifested all those in my life—not through any contrivance—but rather though a real genuine inspection of how I feel and who I am and what I'd like to be and what I like to do.

If I could have one wish, it would be that our traditional Texas culture would remain alive in our ever-changing contemporary society. I think that goes back to when I did a little traveling with the kids when they were young. I never traveled much. I never got out of my environment long enough to really appreciate how unique Texas really is— the manner of dealing—the way the people think, the way they talk, the way they act. The unfortunate thing is that it's being diluted dramatically. This is a natural progression. I lament that, but I'm not bitter about it. It's the natural evolution of any culture in society.

In 1981 I threw my first Texas Independence Day celebration. I have been striving to maintain as much of the traditional culture, the thought, the ideas, and the ideals as much as I possibly can in this ever-changing contemporary society—thus I have put together the Texas Heritage Songwriter Collection. Bob Cole at Hill's Café and I teamed up. This was an original thought to me and he saluted it as a good one to commemorate and try to maintain a touch with Texas culture through its songwriters. They are, in fact, the poets of the common man. They more truly reflect the culture, even more than politicians and others of that ilk. So Hill's is the home place and we have a resolution passed by the state legislature naming Hill's as the home of the Texas Heritage Songwriters Collection. Our whole idea is to recognize not necessarily famous songwriters but those who through their work have preserved and manifested Texas cultural preservation.

We understand Texas might soon have an official
"Outdoor Cooking Utensil." I just knew it was going to be the
Barbeque Pit. Nope. It will be the Dutch Oven.
I just thought I'd be the first to tell you.

PHYLLIS R. MOSES

★ BIRTHPLACE ★
Burleson, TX

★ CURRENT RESIDENCE ★
Georgetown, TX

★ OCCUPATION ★
Historian, Author

When this e-mail came to my website, www.TweedScott.com,

I was immediately taken in by it. Phyllis is an accomplished writer

who knew exactly what I was seeking for this book. Her pride is infectious.

I am Phyllis R. Moses, author and historian. Burleson, Texas, Johnson County is my birthplace. Ft. Worth is the location of my upbringing. We now live in Sun City, Georgetown, Texas and think this is just a foretaste of what heaven will be.

Being a Texan is an evolutionary process. When I grew up, I didn't realize there were other cultures and other states. I particularly didn't know,

We feel that God has transplanted us here for us to observe and enjoy the perfection and beauty of His creation.

couldn't have even fathomed, that other states could make anywhere near the claims we as Texans do about the specialness of our state.

From the regal beauty of the Chisos Mountains and canyons of the Big Bend area, to the high plains of the Panhandle, over to the Piney Woods of East Texas sweep some of the most glorious beauty ever imagined. Then through Central Texas swooping down to the coastal plains of the Gulf Coast area, there are five distinctly different regions of our state. Each has its own peculiar and attractive characteristics. Few states can make this claim. Even transplanted Texans point with authentic pride to the grandeur of our lovely state. Being a Texan is one of the blessings from God that I accept with undeniable acceptance. It doesn't make me arrogant or proud; it makes me grateful.

My favorite place in Texas is where we live now, just on the verge of the Hill Country. We feel that God has transplanted us here for us to observe and enjoy the perfection and beauty of His creation.

The United States Congress readmitted Texas into the Union following the Civil War on March 30, 1870—almost five full years after Lee surrendered to Grant at Appomattox Courthouse.

WILLIAM GOETZMANN, PH.D.

★ BIRTHPLACE ★
Washington, D.C.

★ CURRENT RESIDENCE ★
Austin, TX

★ OCCUPATION ★
Chairman of American Studies, University of Texas at Austin

*I met Dr. Goetzmann through Marshall Kuykendall, another person interviewed
for this book. He provided a more scholarly look at the cause and effect of Texas.
His insight touches upon several points not mentioned by any of the other people interviewed.
He read from a couple of books to get his point across. I couldn't help but get a sense of the
complexity involved in trying to define what Texas is. I came away knowing
there are real reasons as to why certain events shaped Texas and her image.
Yet, I also believe many people's feelings about Texas are based
totally on their perception of it.*

*Dr. Goetzmann grew up in Minnesota and moved to Houston when he was fourteen.
He attended Yale, spent 16 years getting his various degrees and then taught for nine years.
He came to Austin in 1964 to teach at UT. He is the Pulitzer Prize Winning author of*
Exploration and Empire: The Explorer and the Scientist in the
Winning of the American West *(1967).*

I wrote a thing called *Keep the White Light Shining*. I always said that what made Texas "Texas" was enormous space and fundamentalist religion. I'm not so sure that space filling hasn't gained on fundamentalist religion, not being a fundamentalist myself, but still it was the Good Book. Because of the reading of the Bible, and so forth, by so many fundamentalists, Texans are unusually good orators. I've had students who've grown up in Austin who were just marvelous extemporaneous speakers. There's a kind of folklorist quality to it. I admit Lyndon Johnson wasn't very good, but a lot of Texans are very, very good speakers, including our friend Marshall Kuykendall.

Texas was the beneficiary of very sudden wealth. From the time those East Texas oil fields came in, like Spindletop, there was just sudden wealth in East and North Texas where before people had been choppin' cotton and raising sheep. And so they got these oil wells and gas wells and they suddenly got very rich. There was the Dallas wealth. Most of the Houston wealth came from oil wells too. Then, of course, there was cattle, like the King Ranch—big ranches. The cattlemen and the sheep people from Central Texas and the cotton fellows had to work very hard and there were the fishermen in Galveston and Seabrook all the way down the Gulf coast.

So you really had a split in Texas. There was the "big rich" and there was a separation between the merely "well to-do"

and the "suddenly rich". So the suddenly rich bought the ranches, played cowboy and wore their cowboy hats to the State Legislature when they were either lobbying the Texas Railroad Commission so the government couldn't regulate their allowable. It changed the face of Texas both inside and outside. That's part of the Story of Texas too.

A lot of the story of Texas is myth. That's story telling—tall tale telling. I've got a couple of books over here about the humor of the old Southwest. Texas is a part of that southwestern humor and exaggeration. Again, that's part of the reason they're such great orators—the Texas tall tales. Exaggeration of bigness and richness and bravery—it's all very romantic. A lot of people don't believe it but it's fun to hear—more interesting than the tall tales people running for office tell.

Another thing, Texas history is fairly romantic and heroic. How many other states went through that kind of heroic experience? Here was this little, tiny Texas army defeating Santa Anna. The Alamo thing has its heroes although people try to downgrade it. But understand, these guys weren't going to cut and run. And they had chances to. So you have the Texas Revolution, which one writer called the Texan Iliad, and later you had the Mexican War. Then the U.S. Army created all those guys who became heroes in the Civil War. They fought in the Mexican War and they became generals in the Civil War. They had large personalities like Sam Houston and Stephen F. Austin. I keep saying there are only three subjects to write about in Texas history—the Alamo, Sam Houston and the Texas War for Independence. Nobody ever writes about anything else.

Texas had so many cowboys that they became synonymous with the state. Supposedly there weren't any bib overall guys like they have in the Midwest and some of the mountain states and in Oklahoma. Texas had cowboys. They also had Texas Rangers. Texas wasn't hurt by the series of the Lone Ranger. Texas had Indians, though not for long. Texas had Calvary. They had all these colorful people. Again, I think the dividing line came with the oil well. There the Rangers pretty much folded into the Department of Public Safety. The individualism shifted to the oil business. That was when the frontier basically went away.

When I first started teaching here at the University of Texas, students would

> Reading its history is like reading a romance novel.

come with cowboy boots and cowboy hats and stuff to class. I haven't seen one in ten years. I like seeing it. I even like seeing those politician cowboy hats—faux Stetsons. They may be Stetsons but they don't look like real cowboy hats—politician hats. It's like that old expression, "All hat. No Cattle." It's a colorful language that Texans use even if the grammar's strange, usually it's strange deliberately.

We do have some Indian heroes like Quanah Parker. Santana was captured and put in Huntsville Prison. He jumped out of an upper floor because he couldn't stand being jailed anymore—killed himself. There were lots of wild Indians in Texas history. Again the whole state is a romance. Reading its history is like reading a romance novel. Texas was in its own way a crucible. Something special happened here. Texas is, quite possibly, the most envied state.

There are over 200 Lakes and Reservoirs in Texas.
There is only one natural lake—Caddo Lake in East Texas.

DON WATSON

★ BIRTHPLACE ★
New Mexico

★ CURRENT RESIDENCE ★
Canyon, TX

★ OCCUPATION ★
Retired Colonel, U.S. Army

This former career military man proves that Texans just seem to find each other
no matter where they are located. It's tribal. His take on honest-to-gosh
Texas humor proves that some people will never understand Texans—
but that's not necessarily a bad thing.

Texans kind of detect each other. When I was stationed in Bayonne, New Jersey, we ended up having a Texas party, got together and had Mexican food. We just found each other. Maybe it's because we talk funny. You just have a tendency to do that. You pick out other folks from Texas. Even if they are from East Texas—they're still all right. There is a kind of magnetism there somehow.

We lived on a farm in West Texas. I was born in Clovis, New Mexico because that was the only hospital available—it was just across the state line. But I never lived there. We lived on a farm on the Texas side of the line. I lived in NM three or four days. There were six of us and I was the first one born in a hospital. The rest were born at home.

I'm a retired military officer. I teach part time here at West Texas State A&M University. I help them on Saturdays and nights sometimes. I teach an aero-space education class. I retired out of White Sands Missile Range and came back here working in curriculum development for a lot of aviation things back in the Texas Panhandle. I was a Colonel in the U.S. Army. I grad-uated from WT (West Texas State) in '66. They had an aviation cadet program at the time. The Vietnam War was going on. I was going in either as a private or a second lieutenant so I went through the ROTC program. They had an avi-ation cadet program and I ended up staying for it. My career lasted 26 1/2 years. If you notice, the street signs on this campus are named after my classmates that were killed in Vietnam—there were 23 of them. The college was very receptive to that idea because they supported the students—they always have.

It's just a typical West Texas story with cows with horns and helicopters.

◆━━━━━◆

━━◆◆◆━━

Texas is the only state that was once a nation itself. We brag about that some-times. When we were at war with Mexico, Stephen F. Austin said, "Just because we've got the United States on our side this time doesn't mean we can't beat them again."

One time about 15 years ago, I was test flying an aircraft here in Amarillo. Bell Helicopter had a plant rebuilding Vietnam helicopters. I was on an acceptance test flight. Another pilot and I picked up a real vibration in the helicopter. Something was wrong. When Bell produces an aircraft, we test fly it before it goes off to the soldiers. You don't want some guy out of flight school to receive something that might be a problem. So we set it on the ground. Some other test pilots from the company came out and couldn't find what we had found wrong. So they decided to fly it back and crashed it. The problem reoccurred. It did destroy the aircraft and although it didn't kill them, it hurt them pretty badly. The Aircraft Safety Investiga-tion Board came out. They were from like New York somewhere. They came out asking a lot of questions about the air-craft. Since I was one of the two pilots who was flying the aircraft when the problem first occurred, they wanted to know why we had set the aircraft on the ground in a wheat field, radioed for a ground vehicle to come out and pick us up, and shut the aircraft down. They kept pushing as if I should have thrown myself against the skids to keep the other test pilots from taking the aircraft up.

When they pushed that button about the third or fourth time I said, "Let me tell you what really happened. When we set down in this wheat field, once we made our emergency call, a whole herd of cows began to walk to the air-craft and one of them had horns." Well, that was good enough for them. "Gee, I can understand." Yeah, all I had to do was holler "boo" and the cattle would run off. Well, that satisfied those guys. They wouldn't believe the truth. It wasn't our aircraft and I was just trying to stay warm. That's a true story. While everyone was real serious taking notes, all the Texas guys were turning away trying to hide their laughter. It's just a typical West Texas story with cows with horns and helicopters.

There is this magnetism. People knew when I was flying recovery missions in Vietnam that I was from Texas and I wouldn't want to leave anyone ever and they knew that. Somehow they knew that, "West Texas farm kid is going to come get me." Maybe I had some common sense from growing up on a farm.

My dad went through the sixth grade and Mother the tenth. I was the first kid to even go to college. In my dad's time at harvest time, they shut schools down. They had to work. We were sharecroppers. My dad didn't even own the farm. We just rented it. Our rent was a third of the cotton and a fourth of the grain. I couldn't afford to go anywhere other than West Texas State. Came here and got in the ROTC program. What I learned the first six months out of school was that where you went might have made a difference, but after about six months, it didn't. It boiled down to if you could do the job.

I had rather not see another Texan watch me fail than anybody else in the world. You didn't want to let a Texan down. It was just a feeling I had. Strange feeling but it is real. As Texans we have got to shine.

⋯ ⋙✦⋘ ⋯

> You didn't want to let a Texan down. As Texans we have got to shine.

I can remember something called REA (Rural Electric Authority) being at home and being a little ol' kid and I saw something coming way off in the distance for weeks. Dad told me they were stringing light poles. We didn't have electricity. I liked to have worn that string out when we first got electricity. We didn't have running water. I didn't know we were poor. I just didn't know it. We had an old cow for milk, chickens for eggs, and a truck patch for vegetables. We ate well. We didn't have the things others had but we had a closeness in the family and the neighbors down the road were the same way. We'd go work their farm when they were in trouble. It was more of a help-help thing. On a West Texas dry land farm where I grew up, if somebody else was in trouble, you went to help them.

The Panhandle is more of an agrarian area, obviously with lots of cattle and lots of cotton. Oil starts a bit farther south from here but without water, the Texas Panhandle couldn't have existed. There's no big creeks or rivers here. They had to drill for it. So it was a struggle. We had an old squeaky windmill. I can still hear that thing almost. But that was our water. All the time that we had no electricity, we had a windmill. That's where we got our water. I'd go find the little ol' mud cats somewhere and stock our tank with gold fish. It was the only fish I ever saw.

Texans just seem to stay close to each other. Texas has a wonderful history. We took Texas history in high school. I know what "Remember Goliad" means, and, "Remember the Alamo," and all those things. If those people in our state fought that way so can I—even when we're somewhere else.

Texas has 4,959 square miles of inland water,
according to the 2001 U.S. Statistical Abstract.
That is the most of any state in the lower 48.
Minnesota ranks second.

VALERIE BAKER

★ BIRTHPLACE ★
Arlington, TX

★ CURRENT RESIDENCE ★
Canyon, TX

★ OCCUPATION ★
Student, West Texas A & M

You will constantly hear of the friendliness of Texans no matter
where you go in Texas. Valerie Baker told me in a coffee shop in Amarillo,
something of the spiritual side of Texas.

The people make Texas special. I think they're friendlier—whether it's in a city or a small town. We're so laid back and friendly. I was born here but that was my experience. For me, I wouldn't want to live anywhere else but in Texas—maybe not the Panhandle—but in Texas. I like the people and how everyone treats each other nice. It's just really down home. I was raised a lot different than my friends that were born here in Texas and yet you still have the same kind of pride. It's not like I was raised to be, you know, I'm Texas born and raised. I'm proud to be a Texan. It's part of me.

I do notice that we're the only state where a beer or truck commercial has to put in the word "Texas"—"Texas Tough" or something like that. If you go up North it's not going to be like that. It's Texas this and Texas that. So maybe it is psychologically branded into our heads.

I am really proud to be a Texan. It will definitely be my home in my heart but I feel that we're also part of the American way. So I'm also proud to be an American. If I had to move to another state whether by choice or not, Texas will still be home. It's always home. If I was to move to, say, Florida, I would still root for Texas A&M...I would still root for the Cowboys even though they are not doing so good. I will always root for the Rangers. I will always root for a Texas team over any other team. It's home.

To be a native Texan? To me I feel like I'm special. I know that's arrogant to say but to be a native Texan I feel that...I don't know really what it means to me. That's the honest truth. To me being a Texan and also having the opportunity to be born and raised on the border of Arlington and Ft. Worth I've seen the city life, kind of...but it's a more laid back city...not like Chicago or New York. Also moving up to the Panhandle, I also get to see the plains area—everything's flat. The personali-

> Honey, no matter where you go in Texas, you're in the Bible Belt.

ties and people are really different too, but I notice that no matter where you go in Texas, it's really Bible belt. It's kind of weird because people will say, "Oh we're up in the Bible belt here." I'm thinking, "Honey, no matter where you go in Texas, you're in the Bible Belt." It's the same everywhere you go.

The one thing I got from traveling all over the state is everybody is so friendly. They're willing to go out of their way. For example, I was driving to Austin for a funeral from here (Amarillo). It was really, really late. It was almost midnight and I ran over a log on the highway. It bent my rim. I drove through a small town and I don't know why people were up but they were. And I went to a gas station and three gentlemen from that town — one went all the way back home got a hammer and a crowbar— took my tire off, aired it up for me, and put my rim back on so I could make it to Austin. They made sure I was safe and I was OK.

Texas? I love it!

VIVIAN BLOYS GRUBB

★ BIRTHPLACE ★
El Paso, TX

★ CURRENT RESIDENCE ★
Ft. Davis, TX

★ OCCUPATION ★
Retired Elementary School Teacher

Here is another of the pioneers of West Texas. She's been around Fort Davis since the 1930s and has seen the transformation of the community. I couldn't help thinking that the more things change, the more they stay the same.

I'm a third generation Texan. I have lived in Fort Davis most of my life. We were over here so much because my grandmother lived here. I came here when my Daddy was elected county clerk in 1934.

Back then it was more like one big family. If there was anything going on everybody got into it. Now we're divided into churches and it's just not the same and there are so many more people that have moved in that don't take part in anything in town—just retired on these resorts and developments. We've had a drought for so long that the ranchers have sold off their property to developers. We have developments all around town. Just look at the ranches in the last three years that's sold out. They can't afford to feed their cattle because of the drought.

West Texas seems to be pretty quiet most of the time because there's very little social climbin'. There is a group that is like "high society," but Texas as a whole is not that way. I don't think we're so politically involved either. Kinda leave it to do what you think's best. Just kinda laid back.

West Texas has been a little slow for improvement and technology. They just kinda remained cattle, farm, and ranch. It is hard to come in and start. When I was growing up most people had their own garden, their own cows and their own everything but if somebody else needed it, it was shared 'til they got back on their feet.

My grandfather came here in 1888— my husband's grandparents also. In that time Fort Davis was kind of rough. There were the soldiers and there were so many saloons. But when the fort closed, the town was pretty well settled and had moved up this way away from the fort. Maybe Texas has had good missionaries or something or at least it looks like it has. 'Course the only thing I can think of that Texas is really into is football. We're big football fans. It's almost a religion.

I think it's because of the opportunity to get our freedom from Mexico that so many missionaries moved in. Maybe we're a little more conscious that way— in helping each other and being a family.

Well, I don't really know what it means [to be a native Texas]. I'm just proud to

> I just feel safer here for some reason but, of course, this is all I know.

be an American. Maybe it's because of the history of Texas. It has such a history—our history was frontier and really rough. That is one thing why I think we are really close as a people, it's because of the different countries that ruled us. It was because of the different people too, the French, Germans—just every kind. I think the Germans moved in to help the Texans. They really came in droves. The Indian trouble was here so late in the history of the United States too. I guess we were just rough and tumble people. So we do feel close. I think maybe it's just 'cause I live here. We have a little more freedom. I feel like most places in Texas have more law enforcement. I feel safer here for some reason but, of course, this is all I know.

When I was growing up livin' in this triangle of these three little towns—Fort Davis, Marfa and Alpine—that's all we knew. Texans realize that we couldn't have had the freedom if people from all the other states—Crockett and all them, hadn't come in to help. I think we're real grateful people for having what we have. I don't know why we feel so patriotic. It's all about pride. And some of us have too much.

Maybe we just like to brag. There are so many people like myself that are not many generations away from the frontier. We feel what our families lived.

DOUG MORELAND

★ BIRTHPLACE ★
Alpine, TX

★ CURRENT RESIDENCE ★
Austin, TX

★ OCCUPATION ★
Singer, Songwriter and Chainsaw Artist

Doug is an Austin based entertainer with his roots deeply embedded in the
Davis Mountains of far West Texas. His family comes from the pioneer spirit
that still lives there. As an entertainer, he has represented Texas in more places than
I can count. He possesses an infectious personality. You cannot help but like this man.
He understands what being a Texan is all about and is grateful for being born here.

**W**hen I was a kid, I remember thinking, man, I could have been born anywhere. That'da been awful but I was born in Texas—and West Texas to boot. I've lived a lot of different places, 'course, every place I go I get the nickname "Tex." When I lived in Lubbock, everybody called it West Texas. I had to drive five hours northeast to get to it from my hometown so I assumed it was more North Texas. I figure West Texas is Fort Davis, Alpine, and all the way out to El Paso.

I liked growing up having to make up things to do. No video games...no nothing. My mom wouldn't let us play inside if the weather was nice. "Get out-

I've lived a lot of different places, 'course, every place I go I get the nickname "Tex."

side, go do something, make up something to do", she'd say. There's mountains right there. We climb the mountains I built all sorts of forts and played trucks.

My mom's an artist. My dad is too. He plays music and has a little cowboy band. Plays out there and builds wagons. He's really into the western culture. He wishes it was a hundred years ago.

My granny died last year. She'd have been a great one to talk to. She sold ranches and she grew up out there. Her dad grew up out there. His name was Weatherford. His dad founded Driftwood and he was one of the first people to settle where Driftwood is [today]. That's on my Mom's side of the family. Bull Weatherford was my great-granddad and he owned a place outside of Marfa and that's where my granny grew up. She just stuck around there. We go back four or five generations, I guess—on both sides.

My granny went to college at Sul Ross and got kicked out for knockin' out a professor 'cause he gave her an "F". Flat knocked him over his desk and they kicked her out. They had an old Model-T pickup—her and her friends they'd go drivin' around. This was in the thir-ties when they were going to college there. That was the first time they put up street lamps in the parking lots. She had this little sawed off 30-30 with a 14-inch barrel that a guy who worked for Winchester had given to her dad when the gun company was going around at the turn of the century selling and promoting the Winchester. She had that and her friends bet her that she couldn't shoot out all the lights in the parking lot while ridin' around in the back of that truck. She shot them all out. 'Course the next week they put new lights up and they bet her again and she shot 'em out again. Then they didn't have lights up in the parking lot until the 1960s. They just gave up on it. That's the way she tells the story. They never caught her.

There's some kind of pride that goes along with being a native Texan. I don't even know how to define it and I'm sure hardly anybody does. But I can tell you this, I went to South Africa for a month one time just to hang out. They'd ask where I was from and I'd say America and they'd say "blah... American." But if I said Texas, it was completely different. They'd want to talk to me. It was that way everywhere. So I wore my hat proudly everywhere I went over there.

SHERMAN TAYLOR III

★ BIRTHPLACE ★
Taylor, TX

★ CURRENT RESIDENCE ★
near the city of Bastrop, Texas

★ OCCUPATION ★
IT Coordinator at Dell Star Technologies

Sherman is an engaging, exuberant person who was fun to talk with about Texas.
When Sherman talks about the many different aspects of Texas, he exudes all the pride
of being a native. As a native, he makes assumptions that come from knowing you are
somehow a member of a special group of folks. He is an outdoor enthusiast,
so it's easy to see both his attraction to and reverence for the land.
Texas has always been about the land and still is.

Have you ever met a person from Texas that wasn't happy to be from this state? Texas is it's own place, always been it's own place. We are designated as the Southwest but if you really look at it we stick out like a sore thumb. It is the Lone Star State, but it is that feeling of independence.

Right to this day, Texas could sever itself from the Union and we would survive without a problem. If Texas were to pull out of the United States, we would have the seventh or tenth largest economy in the world behind New York.

There is so much diversity in Texas in terms of land and people. Wherever you go in Texas, people are proud to be from Texas. This is a happy place to be. There is a certain pride to the state. You just kind of pick that up—especially if you grew up here or if you have been here for any length of time.

Then there's the majesty and diversity of the state. That is something else to be proud of. You can go from a desert to a swamp inside of ten hours. You can go from South Texas brush country to the Piney Woods forests inside of eight and half to nine hours. There is so much here. Most people don't even know there are mountains in Texas. You have to go west to find them, but they are there. The highest is Guadalupe Peak, which is near nine thousand feet.

> When I die just say a couple of prayers, take the Texas flag and put it at the bottom of my feet.

If you ever drive around the United States people always tell you, especially people from Texas, the only part that is bad about Texas is that it takes so long to get out of the state. Once you get out of the state you are almost there. I have driven to Los Angeles a couple of times. It takes 20 hours to get there from Texas and eight of those hours are getting out of Texas.

I have a game I play when I travel. I count counties. It keeps me occupied to see if I can remember all the counties from the bottom of IH-35 to the top. I usually start at San Antonio and work my way up to Dallas. Then say

them backwards. It helps pass the time, especially when you keep messing them up.

Austin is still Austin. Austin has a very laid back attitude. Most people come to work pretty casual but we know we are the state capital. Austin is so geographically different from other cities. If you look in every direction from Austin it is different. If you go south you start going to San Antonio there is the brush country. If you go west there is the Edwards Plateau. If you go toward Taylor and Granger it is black land prairie. Past that is the Cross Timbers. You get a little of East Texas if you go toward Bastrop. All that is within an hour's drive. That's what makes Austin a great place. People come from everywhere to get to Austin.

Being a native Texan is a sense of pride and ownership. Both of my parents are from towns that don't even have populations now, but it is something when you pass through those towns—the land, the pride of what it represents, how hard they worked in their lifetimes to provide the opportunity that they gave me. The opportunity is here because the land is here. The economy is here. There is always something to do in Texas just because the land itself is there. There is space for everybody. There is enough for everybody to get something. You don't have to fight over it. If you were born here, Texas pride is just born with you.

When I die, just say a couple of prayers, take the [Texas] flag and put it at the bottom of my feet. I already told them. That's the only thing I want. They can have all that other stuff, just put me in a pine box and put the flag at my feet.

~ ~=+=~ ~

STUFF OF LEGENDS

Texas has 90 mountains a mile high or more.
Guadalupe Peak in West Texas is the tallest at 8,749 feet.

About ten percent of Texas is covered by forest.
This includes four national and five state forests.

If you were to walk the border of Texas completely
around the state, you would have walked 3,816 miles.

The border with Mexico, the Rio Grande River, is 1,254 miles.

Texas has three of the ten most populous cities in America—
Houston, Dallas and San Antonio.

The Real Deal

You can always spot a cowboy. He just has a look, a demeanor all his own. You can see it in his face and if you get close enough to see his hands, then any lingering doubts will disappear.

The other day as I was walking into the big discount store, I couldn't help but notice the big chuck wagon display on the parking lot near the entrance selling chili and beef jerky. Several horses were stationed nearby to offer authenticity. It certainly looked like the "real deal."

That's when I spotted him walking towards me. Even before our paths crossed, I was impressed by his full countenance. He was the real deal from head to toe, topped with an impressive well-worn silver felt cowboy hat and blue bandana loosely tied around his neck with a pronounced knot. His neckerchief partially covered the left shoulder of his mid-blue chambray shirt. As he drew closer, I couldn't miss the swaggering gait of his step. He wore a manly, functional buckle that held his plain black leather belt together. His jeans, which showed some wear, were tucked into the tops of his horse-seasoned, bull-hide, reddish-brown high-top boots. Under his nose he sported a fully-grown handlebar moustache centered between the crow's feet between his eyes, above his square jaw.

He was impressive—a real working cowboy. One last pass of the eye revealed this American icon carried a black leather holster on his hip. I looked closer to inspect his choice of sidearm—at that very moment, he went for the weapon and snatched it to the ready in a blink. Fully expecting a quick-draw demonstration, I gazed in amazement as he dialed his phone!

DARRELL K. ROYAL

★ BIRTHPLACE ★
Hollis, Oklahoma

★ CURRENT RESIDENCE ★
Austin, TX

★ OCCUPATION ★
Special Assistant to the President on Athletic Affairs
University of Texas

Darrell Royal is a class act if one exists in the world today.
You're pretty special in Texas when you get a stadium named after you.
Although I had met this Texas legend a couple of times during my radio days,
I can't say I really knew him. He was gracious and generous with his time to talk about
his adopted state. I found him to be warm, funny, and sincere. His passion for Texas
is real and deeply felt. I consider our conversation nothing short of a privilege.

During his 20-year tenure as head coach for the Texas Longhorns, 1957-76,
Royal won four National Titles, 11 Southwest Conference crowns, six straight Cotton Bowl
berths and the so-called Game of the Century when top-ranked UT defeated
No. 2 Arkansas, 15-14. Legend, Icon, Texas Sports Hero—when the name of
former University of Texas head football coach Darrell Royal is mentioned,
those are almost always the words associated with him.

Tweed: In your estimation what makes Texas special?

Darrell: If you take the state in its entirety—just take the lyrics to "Beautiful Texas"…"You can live on the plains or the mountains or down where the sea breezes blow but you're still in beautiful Texas." There's a lot of flat land up in the Panhandle. We've got coastal areas. We've got some mountains and we have some rather large cities—Dallas, Ft. Worth, El Paso, Beaumont-Port Arthur area, Houston, San Antonio. And now, their predicting Austin to surpass San Antonio. So there's a lot of population here and a lot of diverse area. And Texans do have a lot of pride. I like that.

Tweed: Where's that pride come from?

Darrell: I think they get it from their history lessons in school. There's just a lot of pride in Texas. Some outsiders resent it, you know, overly expressed pride. I guess people would resent it. I never have interpreted it that way. Texans take that pride with them.

Tweed: What impact do you think Texas having been its own country has had on that notion?

Darrell: Well, it's the background to the whole thing. You can go to the Bob Bullock Museum and they've got a thing there in the theater that explains Texas beautifully, I think.

Tweed: Texas football is like a religion. Where do you think that came from?

Darrell: I think it comes from heritage from way back. That's why it's good to have a coaching position in the state. There is so much outstanding coaching done in high schools in the state of Texas—and outstanding prospects. In a state this large, you're still recruiting Texans. That's a lot different than recruiting four states. And Texas is about the equivalent of recruiting four states. But there's a difference when you cross the state line and go to recruit a young man from out of state. As a matter of fact, I think, in 20 years we had ten letterman from out of state.

Tweed: From my days spent in Oklahoma, I could tell there was a huge psychological border that started at the Red River. You just knew that rivalry was for real.

Darrell: Oh, was it real! I can tell you, I grew up in Oklahoma and played at Oklahoma.

Tweed: What was it like becoming the Head Coach at Texas with an Oklahoma background?

Darrell: I chose coaching as a profession. It was my job and naturally I do everything I can to have a winning program wherever I would be coaching. I have been asked if I felt different playin' Oklahoma the first time. It was kinda unusual because I played under Coach (Bud) Wilkinson and that was the first time we had ever been in competition. Yeah, it was a little different, but basically I was gung ho for my flag.

Texas is the
total ball of wax.

Tweed: What is it about Texas that grows on you?

Darrell: Well, I just know it's real. I've lived here 47 years. That's way longer than I've lived anywhere. I grew up at Hollis, spent time in the military and four years at the University of Oklahoma. I spent—what—22 years in Oklahoma and I've lived here 47. I have seen some changes here in Austin. The little two lane highways that were out there in the country are now six lanes and full of traffic. But what I'm saying is, I know it's real and why it happens, I don't know. Maybe it's because Texas has lived under six flags. They had the Alamo. There's a lot of things about Texas and the statehood. Think of it—the people and the politicians that have come out of here. Texas is the total ball of wax.

Tweed: What can you say about your friend Willie Nelson?

Darrell: Willie is an extremely loyal person. That fact has been dodged for some reason. If he's your friend, I mean he's a loyal friend. Let me give you an example. We've had a golf tournament—the Ben Willie Darrell (Ben Crenshaw, Willie Nelson, Darrell Royal)—we've had it for 30 years. We started in Galveston. Then we moved to Houston. Then we moved up here to (Austin). Willie made 30. Thirty out of thirty. Now there's no tellin' what that's cost him—givin' up that weekend time. He's just grown. He's done it his way. He sings his way and he picks his way and he's a great writer. It took people a long time to catch on but boy, when they caught on—he's hottern' a match.

Tweed: You know that anywhere Willie goes in the world, he represents Texas.

Darrell: And you know he's going to come back. Well, he's a Texan. Make no mistake about that. And he wouldn't be Willie without Texas."

Tweed: Some final thoughts about Texas?

Darrell: You can tell, I've been vaccinated and dipped.

WILLIE NELSON

★ BIRTHPLACE ★
Abbott, TX

★ CURRENT RESIDENCE ★
Austin, TX (and the road)

★ OCCUPATION ★
Entertainer

*One of the benefits of my 30 years in broadcasting was the opportunity to meet people
I could have only dreamed of meeting when I was a kid. Most of my career found me
in the country music format. I was fortunate enough to meet most of the country
entertainers from the 1970s through the 1990s and beyond. I had met Willie Nelson
several times, but always on the periphery of someone else's conversation.
However, I am fortunate to have a friendship with Poodie Locke, one of Willie's best friends.
While interviewing Poodie and Bobby Boyd for this book, Poodie said,
"You can't do a book about Texas and not have Willie Nelson or Coach Royal in it.
They are Texas." Well, I always wanted to include him, but from my experience,
you just don't pick up the phone and call him—at least I don't.
Poodie said he'd make it happen. Well, it took a while but it did happen.
We did this interview over the phone while Willie was on his bus
headed to Dallas to catch a plane to Scotland.*

What strikes you about Willie is how genuine he is. Like his good friend Darrell Royal,
he was both gracious and generous with his time. He puts you at ease and you immediately
feel comfortable talking with him. He is down to earth and laid back.
You somehow know that if you have Willie for a friend, you have a good friend.
I was especially struck by his sincerity. When I asked him what was special and unique
about Texas, there was total silence for about ten seconds and then he said:

Texas feels like home. Once you call Texas your home, it doesn't matter whether you're born here or not. So, you don't have to be born here to love it. In fact, you might be able to tell more about it by comin' in from the outside. I know a lot of people that wasn't born here that sure look like they love Texas as much as anybody else does. A lot of us just take it for granted. It's all those things people say. And it's all true too, if you have to explain why you like Texas, then why bother? You like it. You got your own ways of explaining why you like it. I can understand why some people get a little upset with somebody who just expects everybody in the world to realize that if you're not from Texas you're different.

The only problems I ever have with anybody is when somebody puts Texas down without knowing anything about it. You know, talking about Texas and cowboys. We've got a little bad press recently about cowboys in Texas. I think that's uncalled for.

I don't know that I have ever thought I was somehow special because I came from Texas. I just know that I feel differ-ent. I used to brag about being able to tell when I was on my bus or in my car—I'd be sleeping in the back or something—and we would leave Arkansas and hit Texas, I'd wake right up. Now roads are just as bad everywhere. Used to be, the old Texas freeways would smooth out. You'd get off the old rough Oklahoma roads and once you got on those big Texas freeways, well then, you knew you was home in Texas. Today those freeways are just as bumpy as they are anywhere. But to a guy who's really from Texas, or really feels like he's from Texas, he's proud of it. I would expect anybody from Rhode Island to feel the same way.

About the people in Texas? Well, I don't know, you know? I travel all over the world and I find friendliness everywhere. I've been to a lot of places where you really didn't expect it but there was. I've been in the middle of two or three wrecks around the world and all of a sudden there are some friends. You feel like, well, these guys could be from Waco. So I just don't know that it's true that we're different. I know we feel different because this is where we're from. Whatever's in our bodies—our DNA—there's an attraction between the ground and the body. I know I feel better when I'm in Texas and it doesn't matter whether it's El Paso or Texarkana or Abbott—just something about being there, it automatically makes me feel better.

Darrell Royal? Coach Royal does know the value of loyalty and friendship. I'd like to think I do too. We've been very close friends for years, so there wouldn't be anything he could ask that I wouldn't do, but I know the same thing applies to him.

What is it that draws people to Texas? I don't know, there's a lot of stories about how great a place it is for one. For the old timers, there was a lot of work down here when there wasn't some work in other places. There's a lot of different things, like climate. You can't say that everybody in Texas is a nice guy either. I know some bad [people]—men, and women, and children. So you cannot say everybody from here is perfect.

You say I'm synonymous with Texas but I don't really feel a role or pressure, but I do feel like I represent Texas and I do travel around the country a lot. We see a lot of people. We drop the Texas flag every night on stage no matter where we are, whether we are in Austin or Australia. So, we're proud to be from Texas and we don't mind people knowin' about it. So yeah, I like to think we are good ambassadors—not only me but Poodie and the gang. People look forward to us dropping the flag every night now.

The mothers and daughters of Texas who go all the way back to the beginning, probably have as much if not more pride than anybody. And rightfully so. My parents and grandparents came from Arkansas. They came down here and started a garage and a blacksmith shop in Abbott. I was born in 1933, so they hadn't been here that long before I was born. So a couple of years difference one way or the other, I could've been from Arkansas—which ain't no bad deal either. I was driving through Arkansas the other day and saw a big sign for a tourist attraction for Hurricane Cave. I thought to myself, "When's the last time they had a hurricane in Arkansas?" We laughed about that for a few miles.

> Texas feels like home. Once you call Texas your home, it doesn't matter whether you're born here or not.

WILLIAM JAMES "BILL" LEFTWICH

★ BIRTHPLACE ★
Duncan, OK

★ CURRENT RESIDENCE ★
Ft. Davis, TX

★ OCCUPATION ★
Freelance Artist, Sculptor and Writer

~ ❖ ~

Bill Leftwich has written eight books. He is a lecturer to elder hostel groups
on the history of the Southwest and Mexico. I was later told that during WWII,
he also served as a tank driver for General George S. Patton. He's as dynamic as
his sculptures and as colorful as his artwork. He is a living history. He started our
conversation by talking about a particular ranch and made reference to its size.
He said it was 2.4 RI. What on earth?... It took me a moment to realize what he was
telling me. The ranch was the size of 2.4 Rhode Islands. I could see the
amusement in his eyes and by the broad smile on his face, I knew I had been had.
You cannot help but get a real sense of how tough it was to live in Texas.
It can be an unforgiving place. You have to respect your surroundings.

A Texan knows he's part of something special.

My grandfather had the first store in Lawton, Oklahoma. He took a team and wagon and put up a tent in Lawton. He and a fella named McCaslin put in a grocery store there. They came over from Duncan. All the Indians from the area used to come over—Quanah Parker and Ishati and all those others used to come over and trade in Duncan.

Spain invaded Mexico in 1519 and started colonizing it in 1521. Two centuries later there were only 2,500 people in Texas. They couldn't get people to leave Mexico, cross the Rio Grande and come into Texas even though they owned it because of the Indians—the Comanche, the Apaches and other Indians. No one wanted to come in here so they established a fort and a church at Nacogdoches to keep the French out. Mexico also established San Antonio and the Alamo and various other missions. They provided a military force and they had ranches along the Rio Grande and on the Gulf Coast but they only had 2,500 people.

So in order to try and keep the French from coming in and to finally eradicate the Indians, they opened it up for immigrants from the United States. They said if you will swear to be citizens of Mexico and swear to be Catholic—of course the Baptist and the Church of Christ crossed their fingers—they'd give 'em land grants. Now it was around Gonzales where Stephen F. Austin got the first land grants. They

were adventurous people. When the Anglos finally had their war against Santa Anna, they didn't really intend to make Texas a republic. They wanted Santa Anna to honor the Constitution of 1824, when Mexico formed its republic. It took Mexico three hundred years to get independence from Spain—from 1521 to 1821. In the first

A Bill Leftwich original

two years they had an Emperor, then in 1824 they formed a constitution similar to ours and a government like ours. But Santa Anna didn't pay any attention to it. So the Texans got the idea "Let's just break away and form a republic." And that's what they did. The fact that they had the gall and the nerve to do that gave all of us a sense of pride and maybe the big head to where we think that we can tackle anything. We've just got an attitude. That stems back to that kind of start.

This part of Texas [the Big Bend area] started when they put the forts in here because of immigrants going to the gold rush in California and also to protect the stagecoaches that were coming through. We had a stagecoach line from Missouri all the way to San Diego. It came down through Fort Worth and it went out West. The Comanches and Apaches would raid those and kill those people so they put the forts out in 1854—Fort Davis here.

> That's two things we have: wind and sunshine.

After the war with Mexico in 1846-48, some Anglo stayed at Presidio. And then a man from Missouri came out named Milton Favorite. He'd shot a man back in Missouri and thought he'd killed him, but he didn't. The guy got over it. At least he lived awhile after that. Now Favorite came down here and started ranching and established some forts that were his ranch head-quarters—three different ranches down below Marfa. That was the first agriculture out here.

The people who came to the Trans-Pecos area were tough people. They needed more land and kept moving west. It was hard. A lot of them were killed by the Indians. There were rustlers too. There was always trouble with raiders from across the Rio Grande. But they were tough people and endured it all.

An annual rainfall of nine inches or less is considered desert. At our altitude, here in the Davis Mountains, we should get around fifteen each year. Most of the Trans-Pecos is desert—Chihuahuan Desert. So it's a hard country. The advent of the windmills really did help the Trans-Pecos where we could ranch nearly any of it.

It also helped the wildlife because it gave them more water in places. The water table depends upon where you are. My well is at 150 feet. The water came up to 90 feet. That was 25 years ago and that hasn't changed. Now they're doing solar here. They have been very successful—cheaper than a windmill. If you have a ranch and you're twenty miles from a power line, it will cost you a bundle to try and get electricity out there to it. So it's better to just get you a solar powered pump to put on that well. We've got lots of sunshine. No shortage of that. They're really trying to perfect the mechanical part of the windmills to where they will be efficient. We do have the wind. That's two things we have: wind and sunshine.

I talked to Moroccan soldiers in World War II that was on a bridge with me one time. They wanted to know where I was from and I said, "Texas." Oh man. They started making motions like they were whippin' their horse and ringin' out their six guns. They knew exactly what I was talking about.

My brother tells people that when he went into the army, our dad said, "Now son, when you tell people you're from Texas, don't ask where they're from. There's no need to embarrass them."

One thing about this area here [Fort Davis]—we've always had problems with Mexico. During the revolution—1910–1920—they'd come across and raid ranches and kill people. But now most of our population here is Mexican. We're probably 60 percent in town and I know all of them. We're all good friends.

There was not enough military or enough state lawmen or local law to protect everybody so out here they were gun-toters. They had Winchesters and single action Colts and they had to take care of themselves. That hasn't changed a whole lot. And when these gun control people come up and say you can't buy such and such type ammunition or you have to register when you buy a gun and things like that, it just galls us to no end because all of us like to have a pistol or rifle handy and still do. It was a way of life. You had to rely on yourself. That's one reason why we are gun nuts out here—at least most of the men are. Guns were one of your tools for living. It hasn't changed a whole lot.

One thing they say about Big Bend is it has lots of places where you can be by yourself. What they mean is that you better be careful and don't get lost 'cause you may die out there if don't have enough water. You could be by yourself for eternity. I was a ranger down there in the summer of 1953 advising people to have hats and carry plenty of water. That was the main thing I told them. A lot of people come from East and they don't realize how quickly dry country down there with 10 or 15 percent humidity can dry a person out. So you needed a couple of gallons of water every day.

There is one other thing I would add. People that went to A&M, like I did in 1941, had to want to go there. Once you finally graduate, there's a certain spirit at Texas A & M that is part of the Texas spirit. A & M belongs to all of Texas and although we have a running fight with the University (UT), it's mainly in fun. It's a good university and we know that. Being a Texas Aggie and being from Texas gives you a sense of pride that only Aggies and Texans have. I know a lot of people will laugh at that but they just don't know. A Texan knows he's part of something special.

LIZ CARPENTER

★ BIRTHPLACE ★
Salado, TX

★ CURRENT RESIDENCE ★
Austin (Westlake), TX

★ OCCUPATION ★
Author and Former Press Secretary for First Lady, Lady Bird Johnson

As I sat in Liz's home, I was overwhelmed by a sense of history.
This woman was the press secretary to a First Lady, Lady Bird Johnson.
I had often observed her at a distance. I came close to meeting her several times
at the Texas Book Festival in Austin where I have been a volunteer for several years.
As fate will have it—and fate will have it—I knew someone who had done some work
with her. I was surprised when I asked my friend how to get in touch with Liz and she said,
"Look her up, she's in the phone book." I did and she answered the phone.
We set up an appointment, and within a day or two, I was sitting in her office.
She continued working on some papers while she talked to me. I found her to be
a totally upfront, tell-you-like-it-is, look-you-straight-in-the-eye Texan.
One of the reasons I wanted to talk to her was even though I had never met her before,
she had always struck me as being a person who came from real pioneer stock.
I wasn't wrong.

I was born in the family home place in Salado, Texas—a tiny town in central Texas that was once considered to be the capitol. It had an early college there—you'll find crumbling walls on the hill. Later that college became what really amounted to a very upgraded high school. My mother and father went there. I placed a bench there on that hill in their memory and that is where I will be strewn when I go on to that great Democratic convention in the sky. I'm planning to have my ashes mixed with wildflower seeds. It's a beautiful hill that overlooks the main street. It has my great grandfather's statue standing on it because he was a very early settler. It's just a charming place that looks across at Stagecoach Inn. It's about a seven-acre park that's run by the Central Texas Area Museum.

I grew up very blessed having lots of stories told around the fireplace about Texas. Both my mother's family, which was named Robertson (Sterling Robertson) and my father's family (Thomas Sutherland) got into Texas before 1836, which marks the time of our revolution. So if you lived in Texas at that time, there were about 28,000 white people—the only ones they counted. You were part of the fighting or part of the writing. I have ancestors who were part of both. It was always a matter of great pride to my family. We are a close-knit family. We have been having family reunions for 75 years as the Sutherlands. I am a sixth generation Texan.

In the house where I was born, which was built in about 1852 with 24 rooms and no baths at that time, there was a 'strangers room' on the front of it that did not empty into the house. It only emptied to the outside. Anybody who was riding through could stop, unsaddle their horse and sleep there. Often they were invited for dinner because people were hungry for conversation. So the 'stranger's room' really says something about Texas. I also think that space and blue skies have made Texans friendly—friendly beyond repair. I think that comes from the size of the state—land to roam gives us freedom and a sense of needing each other.

I think that we have always needed each other. We had a high risk economy from the beginning. Cattle could roam and they could stampede so you needed some neighbors who would help you. An oil well could come in and blow its top. We had trees that could be ruined. These were high risk things. But Texans like that challenge and that was what was available. You did know that you needed your neighbor.

Jim Michener came here to write about Texas. He said it was the first time that he had gone anywhere and people came up to him that had a real sense of personal possession about their stories. They told him you've got to use the Sam Houston soup story. He said he had been told the story about seven times before he arrived. They would tell a story about their own family. There is this close tie to Texas. We don't want anybody to miss out on what makes us like we are.

The way the soup story goes is that one time while dining, Sam Houston was telling a story as he was served some soup that was boiling hot. Not paying attention, he took a spoonful of it and sputtered it all over the table. Everyone at the table waited for the great Houston to apologize for his actions. Instead he just said, "A damned fool would have swallowed that." Well, that's very Texas. It also said a lot to James Michener about the kind of people we are.

Space, blue skies, and white caliches soil—all of those are a part of Texas. We have also been strong for the underdog because we could have been there ourselves. I think it's the most likeable state because of the people who live here. As people, we are shaped by our surroundings and by the conditions. We don't feel lined up or pressed because of all that space. Some of that may be changing as we are invaded by Yankees, so to speak. We allow everybody to claim being a Texan. We allow them to pick up our habits—bragging or truth—whatever you want to call it.

We are close to our history and there are a lot of resources. There are a lot of books written about our Texas history. I was very honored to find out that when they went through the Bob Bullock Museum, someone called and said, "Your family Bible is over here." Sure enough, Major George Sutherland,

> I also think that space and blue skies have made Texans friendly— friendly beyond repair.

who came in here in 1829 brought the family bible. It's there. It's open.

There are a lot of personal possessions that people have hauled down from the attic—old letters and such. There is great interest in historical societies in small towns in Texas in trying to tell the story of how that particular area evolved. We still have, not in our family's possession but in the state archives, a letter written by my great-great grandmother Francis Sutherland to her sister back in Tennessee, dated June the sixth 1836. It says, "Alas poor William". That's her seventeen year old boy. He died at the Alamo on the sixth day. And there is a personal story of a woman describing her son's going down to the Alamo when William B. Travis rallied the troops in and then serving and dying there. There are just countless stories like that. Part of it is we just saved those things. A lot of them are coming down out of the attics in old candy boxes of Texas.

The story of Elizabeth Ney is coming in piece by piece. The Austin History Center really has it. You can go down there and read letters from her. She came from Germany in the last part of the 1800's. I'd classify her as the first liberated woman in Texas, used her maiden name though she was married to a doctor. She was already a recognized and able sculptress. She bought a house out here in Austin that still stands and it is charming. You go into it and you can feel her presence. She built that house where she entertained, supposedly, from her hammock serving clabber, which must have been a first cousin to yogurt. She was everybody's favorite dinner partner. She rode a horse astride, which was not the habit of women of that day. And she wore black clothes. She also won the commission to sculpt two figures to be placed in Statuary Hall in Washington, D.C. She did life-sized figures of Stephen F. Austin and Sam Houston. [Copies of those statues reside at the entrance to the Capitol Rotunda in Austin.] There were complaints that the statues were not the same size. Her answer was, "God made the men, not I." She didn't back down a bit. Ney also received a lot of bills that she couldn't pay. She wrote a letter to the editor of the Austin paper, since she could not pay the bill. She wrote, "Sorry. No money." Those letters are on display at the Elizabeth Ney Museum.

The Texas State Cemetery is full of heroes and scoundrels and some of them are in the same grave. A lot of people were moved there from other places in 1936 when we celebrated our hundredth birthday. You have J. Frank Dobie and [Walter Prescott] Webb. My brother is buried near them. It's a marvelous mix of people. One thing that I think got us all interested in history was on the hundredth birthday of Texas in 1936—I don't know whether it

> It's great to know your roots—to know what you've got there.

was Texaco or Mobil—but they put out a cartoon book of the history of Texas, telling it with sketches and it was really invaluable. Kids loved it and read it. It told about Goliad, and the excitement of our getting our independence. You grew up knowing a lot of Texas history. You studied it in school. It's great to know your roots—to know what you've got there.

We belonged to Mexico originally. Then there were the impresarios who brought colonists down because Mexico wanted Texas to get settled—not everyone agrees to why. Some people believe it was to get the Indians out. A lot of people came in the early days like the Stephen F. Austin Colony and then the Sir Robertson Colony that has what is now nineteen counties.

There were settlers from all over. One of the places you see this is on March 2nd when the Daughters of the Republic have their ceremony there at the Alamo. They call the roll of the names of the people who fought there and the states and countries they were from. I think that Travis was 28 or 32 (years old) at the time, but he was a brash young man who was the leader there. His letters from the Alamo are very appealing and are often read when Texans get together to celebrate the occasion.

Being a Native Texan is what shapes you. There's a fierce independence. Out of it came confidence and all the qualities that go into being a Texan. Part of it was that you were surrounded with people who were, at that time unnamed, mentors. Sam Houston is still quoted, often misquoted by political candidates, "Do right and take the consequences." Because we have grown up with this kind of thing we have our heroes and they are not forgotten. You know your identity in most cases. I really worked hard on that because my own children were raised in Washington. I wanted them to know their history. The two great aunts worked so hard to get the women's right to vote in Texas—this was two years before it was ratified nationally. I had a great uncle who died at the Alamo—two great-great grandfathers who stood with Houston at San Jacinto—I hope that means something to them. I've certainly tried to translate it to them, but I can't ask them to feel it as deeply as I do because they grew up in a faster world away from Texas.

It's true that very few people can say they had relatives at both the Alamo and San Jacinto. I feel embarrassed when I mention that because I think people will think I'm bragging. It is a distinctive thing that's like a feature story about you. It means a lot to me. In your veins, you think, perhaps there's more courage because of them and more independence.

Being a native Texan makes you steadfast in your appreciation of it. My mother gave us two admonitions—make something of yourselves and try to see the humor in a situation. People who are crowded don't know how to laugh. Texans grow up with a kidding streak, perhaps because of the distances between us. I grew up here and have been on the front line of political action for a long time. I've said in several speeches that I never saw a Republican until I was about twenty-one. We pointed to them as strange objects.

Look at how many Texas presidents we've had. There was "Ike", we claimed him although he's buried in Abilene, Kansas, but he was born in Dennison. We had LBJ. We have had other presidents who were imports, George H. Bush 41 and George W. Bush 43. All of them want their Presidential libraries in Texas. They took Texas to their hearts. Of course they made their money here too, in most cases.

BOBBY BOYD

★ BIRTHPLACE ★
Dunlap, Tennessee

★ CURRENT RESIDENCE ★
Spicewood, TX

★ OCCUPATION ★
Singer/Songwriter

POODIE LOCKE

★ BIRTHPLACE ★
Waco, TX

★ CURRENT RESIDENCE ★
Spicewood, TX

★ OCCUPATION ★
Poodie's Hilltop Café, Spicewood, TX

This interview just happened. I agreed to meet Bobby Boyd at Poodie's Hilltop Café
to interview him for this book. He introduced me to Poodie and suggested he join us.
We settled in and talked over a couple of cold brews. Little did I know at the time
that this conversation would have me crossing paths with Darrell Royal,
Kinky Friedman, Willie Nelson and the Alamo movie set.

I first met Bobby Boyd at one of Terry Boothe's Texas Independence
Day celebrations. I was taken by what a great entertainer he is.
Before the day was over, I decided I was going to write a magazine story
for Countryline Magazine *about him. Bobby has a passion for Texas.*
He wrote a song that, as of this writing has never been recorded for release,
is called "I Wasn't Born In Texas But I Got Here As Quick As I Could."
He was kind enough let me include the lyrics in the book.

As far as this particular interview goes, we recorded it at Poodie's Hilltop Café,
which is fun place to catch a variety of Texas performers.
It's an intimate place to listen to Texas music. Poodie cuts to the chase
in this interview. We began by talking about Boyd's song about Texas,
I Wasn't Born In Texas But I Got Here As Fast As I Could...

 **oodie:** Good Song. The first line of the song makes the whole song. "I know a place where the sun sets and paints a rainbow across the sky."

Tweed: What makes Texas so special?

Poodie: It's self-sufficient. We produce our own food, make our own oil...we can grow anything here.

Bobby: And make our own music.

Poodie: Yeah, make our own music, make our own meat, make our own plastics...whatever we need. We're the only state that can still secede from the union.

Bobby: They're a proud people.

Tweed: Where does that come from?

Poodie: We're rugged.

Bobby: I'll tell you where it comes from— I think it's inherited.

Poodie: It was a tough country to live in. When people moved here, until they had air conditioning and reliable water, it was tough living down here.

When it's 118 degrees in Texas, it's hot. It is not a dry heat.

And to start with, it's one of the only states where you have to take Texas history in school. It's instilled in you when you're two years old or three or five when you start school. When you take Texas history you learn how proud Texas people are of their state. You don't go through Connecticut or New Jersey or Vermont and see them hangin' the flag out do you? You can't drive five miles in this state without seeing a Texas flag on somethin'.

Tweed: What about her people?

Poodie: They're rugged. The pride's instilled from birth. When you're a little kid down here you're the best at this or the biggest in that. We have football teams. You look a man dead in the eye.

Bobby: But they're still peaceful people.

Poodie: But they're a proud people. When you shook my granddaddy's hand you looked him right straight in the eye. It's a pride like nowhere else in the world. It's a country in itself.

Bobby: They still stop on the side of the road to help you out down here.

I Wasn't Born in Texas
(But I Got Here as Quick as I Could)
Written by: Bobby Boyd

I know a place where the sunset paints a rainbow across the sky
Where the moon in all it's splendor puts a gleam in every pretty girl's eyes
Where the women love their outlaws like every good cowgirl should
No...I wasn't born in Texas, y'all, but I got here as quick as I could.

chorus
God bless Texas
Where the pretty blue bonnets grow
Where every day there's a rodeo
A juke box and sawdust floors
I've been around the world and I've never found
A place that makes me feel this good
No...I wasn't born in Texas, y'all, but I got here as quick as I could.

spoken verse
Ya' know I've seen a lotta' pretty places in my time
and some faces I'll never see again
But I swear to my soul the Texas Hill Country I know
Is as close to heaven as I've ever been
And I swear I've never seen a prettier woman than I
Have way down in ol' San Antone
But you see that's just one more reason I've got
To make Texas my new home

chorus
bobby boyd music/BMI

Music is a big part of Texas.
That's why a lot of people come to Texas.

Poodie: Well, they're hospitable people—people who'll pull over on a two-lane highway and let you by. They're a friendly sort but, by God, you better watch out. We don't condone violence but we will indulge in it.

Bobby: You know when you go overseas and they ask you where you're from you say, "Texas". You don't say, "United States".

Poodie: Yeah, and if you're from Texas they are going to ask you questions. They don't say, "Tell us about Jersey or South Carolina." People are just fascinated with all the history—the cowboys, Texas Rangers, movies. They're likely the most highly respected law enforcement officers in the world.

My dad had vending machines in Waco. It's where they used to take cattle across the Brazos River. All the cattle herds that came up from the south they had to go across at Waco because that was the only expansion bridge they had. That's why Waco was such a rough town—all these cattle herds would get backed up in Waco. Here's all these cowboys drunk as *&*^%* every night. When I was a kid they used to call Waco "Two-gun Junction." The name of the newspaper was the Inquirer. I know the history of Waco because my grandmother used to have a boarding house

for 45 years right across the street from Waco High School. Waco was the headquarters of the 'F' troop of the Texas Rangers.

A place you need to go is Riemer's Ranch to look at that *Alamo* [movie] set. Actually go into the Alamo mission, it will give you a different perspective. It will give you an idea of what they were up against. When you go to the Alamo in San Antonio, that's the actual mission—the top of that thing wasn't built until 1910. The movie set is all built to scale. You see how big a fort they had. When we were down there, a lot of the guys had studied and done research on it. For one thing, in the first attack on the Alamo, the Mexicans had tall single rung ladders that were about a foot and a half over the wall. So the Texians would push the ladders away from the walls. The walls were two and half feet thick. They could knock down the ladders without being exposed. The Mexicans went back and figured that out and cut the ladders short—so they were just little ways from the top of the wall. The Texians couldn't reach over and push them away without exposing themselves to the gunfire. They couldn't keep the Mexicans from coming—except to throw things down on them—which they did until they ran out of stuff. You get a different perspective and respect for what happened there.

Bobby Boyd

Poodie: Just think of all the country singers that have been here the last hundred years who were from Texas, singers or entertainers. Think of it: Ernest Tubb, Hank Thompson, Buddy Holly, Waylon Jennings, Willie, George Jones, Ray Price, hell, you can go on and on.

Bobby: Well, music is a big part of Texas. That's why a lot of people come to Texas.

Poodie: I've never seen a list of all the singers and songwriters who came

from Texas. Look at Don Henley, Rodney Crowell, the list goes on and on...Bobby Boyd.

Bobby: Now. Have you heard the song "The Ghosts of the Alamo" that I wrote? If you've heard it, you'd a remembered it.

Tweed: What brought Bobby to Texas?

Bobby: The people probably—people and the weather and music, of course. I think it's the people. I'm from Tennessee. I could go past the Tennessee line and people talk different than I do. I come to Texas and hell, people talk like I do. Half of them are from Tennessee anyway. You know, "T" for Texas, "T" for Tennessee. Of course, Willie Nelson—you say the word Texas, you might as well say Willie Nelson along with it.

Poodie: Well, he might head the list but it wouldn't take long to call the roll.

Bobby: I went huntin' out in West Texas and it is completely different than East Texas. The east part of Texas is different. East Texas is like the Old South. In some ways it's almost like Tennessee. I wrote a song called "Behind the Piney Curtain" about East Texas. I'm gradually trying to write songs about different parts of Texas.

Poodie: Yeah, South Texas and the Valley, that's a completely different world. I've got a friend who has a 60,000-acre ranch down there. They are their own law. There's one game warden down there. There's one sheriff. There are six highway patrolmen. It's the whole county.

Bobby: It's just mind boggling to have that much land.

Tweed: Liz Carpenter made the statement to me that the Texas State Cemetery was full of heroes and scoundrels.

Poodie: And most of the heroes were scoundrels.

Bobby: Well, I left the music business in Nashville to come here. It's my second chance.

Tweed: How did Texas influence your songwriting, Bobby?

Bobby: Just the presence, the being around people that I can relate to as far as music goes. They're everywhere. Well, we did the Blues song of the year and I wrote it with W. C. Clark, another guy born in Texas. Just people like Poodie. Hey, you can't get rid of people like him. Hell, they just grow on you. They're unique personalities and I love it 'cause I'm that way anyway.

Poodie: Texans are strong willed, a lot of soul, deep in faith, witty with a little bit of attitude. Yeah, a little bit of attitude and a lot of altitude. Never back 'em in a corner. If you want to get something done, tell 'em they can't do it. Now that's Willie Nelson.

I went to work for Willie 30 years ago. The first gig I did with him was at the Troubadour in L.A. It was a showcase club. We were showcasing the *Red-headed Stranger* album. I drove down Santa Monica Blvd and found a flag store. It had one Texas flag about this big [about a foot square]—the only one they had in the shop. I pinned it up right behind Willie straight up and down. The bigger Willie got—the bigger the flag got. Now we've got one 60 by 40. It's a big one.

Tweed: Explain Willie's his success.

Poodie: He's a people's person. That's why he signs autographs for two and half hours. That's why he does three-hour sets. Whether it's one person or a hundred-thousand it's still the same show. He only sings for one. Whoever

The Ghost of the Alamo
Written by: Bobby Boyd

As my body weak and weary; Meets the stars up in the sky
The beauty of this moment; Slowly closes my eyes

As I tumble into darkness; I see visions of souls
My spirit's there among them; I'm the Ghost of the Alamo

chorus
We have lived and we have died
On freedom's wings, faces in time
Remember me, never let go
I am the Ghost of the Alamo

I can hear the screams of courage; As we stand upon the wall
The men who fought so gallantly; The bravest of them all

As the sword of death cuts through me; A page in history unfolds

My spirit's there among them; I'm the Ghost of the Alamo

chorus

bobby boyd music/BMI

else comes with them, it's better. He'll always find one person in the crowd and have people relate to him. Ask anybody in the first twenty rows—he sang to all of them. In fact, you look up there in the third deck someone will say, "Hey, he looked at me—he waved at me." Sometimes people don't have anybody to hold on to or look up to or believe in. He's just one of those kind of people. He'll look you in the eye and he's got that great smile. Ya know?

Tweed: Any parting shots?

Poodie: If you're not here by now, don't come. We've got enough. The flies are huge and it's too damned hot to live and the water's sour.

Bobby: The women are ugly and the liquor is hot.

Poodie: The mosquitoes and flies are as big as a horse.

Texas is the nation's leading producer of oil, natural gas, beef, sheep, goats, wool, cotton, rice...and, oh yes, watermelons.

MARGE MUELLER

★ BIRTHPLACE ★
Luckenbach, TX

★ FINAL RESTING PLACE ★
Luckenbach, TX

★ OCCUPATION ★
Sheriff of Luckenbach, TX

Marge Mueller, the Sheriff of Luckenbach—really one of a kind—the face of Luckenbach,
Texas. In the course of our conversation, I learned more about Luckenbach than is probably
written in any book anywhere. I was struck by the pride she felt about her
German heritage and the special place Luckenbach holds in the hearts of
all those who visit there. You couldn't help but love her.
She loved what she did. She joked with me that although she had never traveled
the world, she didn't need to because the world came to visit her at Luckenbach.
Marge explained how Luckenbach became a destination for people all over the world.
You can feel Marge's pride as she expresses her thoughts about her home
and her relationship with Texas. She had been blessed and she knew it.

Everybody's somebody
in Luckenbach.

This area was settled in that 1849 to 1850 span. It was then known as the Grape Creek community. The Grape Creek Post Office ran from 1857 to 1868. Then it shut down. The Engels came into the area in 1885. They opened up a new Post Office in 1886 and called it Luckenbach, Texas. My great, great grandfather was the first Luckenbach Postmaster. His name was August Engel. His sister, Minoch, was in here with him and she married a gentleman by the name of Albert Luckenbach. They named the place after him. His brother, Uncle Adolph, was the first bartender. That was across the street from here. Then they had the general store and later on when Ms. Engel and her husband moved out, Uncle Adolph sold out. They needed to move it into one unit, so they moved the bar out of there and put it in here.

My great, great grandfather opened the post office and his son William was the next postmaster, and Beno, he was the last Postmaster they had. By 1970, Uncle Beno had been real ill for a couple of years with emphysema and breathing problems. His children weren't interested taking over a little ol' country store which nobody but the general public visited, you know.

Farmers and ranchers around there they'd come over here and drink a couple of beers after they got through working and played dominoes and cards. Then they'd go home and he'd close up about nine or ten. When Uncle Beno put it in the paper, "Town For Sale," Guich Koock called Hondo Crouch and said, "Hey, why don't we buy Luckenbach?"

Hondo said, "Oh I don't know. You say we can buy the whole thing? OK." So Guich said he talked Hondo into it. "Heck, we can make the payments on it with the eggs we buy and sell."

They couldn't have, but it was a story, you know? So they bought the place. Hondo put up the money and Guich put up the work end of it. They negotiated to where he was going to be the working end and Hondo was going be the financier. It started out like that and four years later in 1974, Guich sold out. He went on to pursue a movie career and TV. He had his fun while it lasted and did play on that Carter Country show.

The year of the World's Fair—about 1973—is when it got started here about people knowin' about Luckenbach. We had about 22,000 people in two days. We had arts & crafts and good music. There was a little carnival for the kids. It started on a Friday and dwindled out on the Sunday.

Then Jerry Jeff (Walker) recorded his first album, *Viva Terlinqua*, here in 1973. So we had a big concert that weekend after he finished his recording. The dancehall was so packed a mouse couldn't have got through. It was so full. Jerry Jeff and his wife got married here in '74. Then in 1976, we had a non-bicentennial celebration. It was called that for the simple reason that Hondo said he didn't appreciate the fact people were rippin' off the American public selling red, white, and blue stuff.

Two guys from Tennessee had heard about Luckenbach and when Jerry Jeff went up there they asked him if he had heard about this little place. They had heard that there were people starting to do some music things around there in Austin and this little place called Luckenbach. Bobby Emmons and Chip Moman, they wrote the song, *Luckenbach, Texas* (The Basics of Love). They ran into Waylon and asked him if he knew about Luckenbach and Hondo and all that stuff. They wanted to know if he wanted to sing the song and put it on an album. And that's what he did. That was in late 1977 or early 1978.

It's funny how I heard about that song. Somebody called down here on the phone and said, "Marge, did you know that they have a song about Luckenbach? They're playing it over the radio right now." I said, "You've got to be kidding. I've never heard anything like that before." He held that phone up to the radio and they were playin' it and that's how I heard about it the first time. I heard it right here off the phone while I was bartending. It sounded like a good song 'cause it really is a nice dance tune. Has a lot of meaning in it. It had the feeling of Luckenbach.

Luckenbach is not as wild as it once was. It was kind of like that at first but now it's mellowed to where it's a really neat place. Luckenbach has an ambiance beyond compare. When you walk on the grounds something kind of

> When you walk on the grounds something kind of grabs a hold of you.

They're trying to find a place where they can kick back and be themselves.

grabs a hold of you. People come in here and they go, "You know, we were going to stop by here and drink one

beer. Here even at nine at night, we've had more than one beer and we're still here. It's like a magnet." They'll say they've had more fun.

So many people come through here and they hit this place last—we had one couple come in and they said, "Marge, you know, we've had two weeks of vacation. We've been traveling all over the state of Texas and we stopped here last. You have made our whole day today. Right here. It's just wonderful." People are so wonderful. You know why? Because they come out here where they don't have to compete with anybody and all of a sudden they are not inhibited. They're just themselves. You really get the feeling like the bumper sticker says: "Everybody's somebody in Luckenbach."

Where else can you find so many different musicians? They play together and they all sit together. It's like they've been practicing with each other for the last sixteen years. And some of them have never been here before. They all just fit together like a jigsaw. I just think people are looking for people, looking for tranquility in all that's going on in the world. They're trying to find a place where they can kick back and be them-

selves. Some people that live out of state, they come down here once a year and go, "Marge we had to come back again because we have to get a grip of reality. Real reality! We have to come back down to earth so we can maintain the next 365 days."

We had bikers from all over the United States. We had a bike rally—like 500 to 1,000 bikes or more—and had no problems. There is a respect out here and everybody "gets it."

Why is Texas unique? There's lots of stuff for tourists. And the tourists are going around saying, "Texas is so beautiful and the people are so wonderful. We've never been treated so well." They talk about the state saying things like, "Texas has the best roads." I think our forefathers who settled here in this part of the United States were all dreamers and believers. They saw great possibilities in this area. The country has everything. Anything you can find in the whole United States, you can find in Texas. Everything! That is probably one reason why it's special. It's because God put everything right here in one little ol' spot and later on the people called it Texas. We got spoiled.

From what I understand, Texas is the only state that is legally allowed to secede if we want to. It's unique. People in Texas are unique. They love who

they are. They love where they were born. They take pride in their families. You see so much pride in them. We have about a hundred-mile span here where all the German settlers came into Texas. All German areas. Of course that's faded some now but even during World War II, they couldn't knock us down because we refused to not be ourselves. Just because they said we weren't allowed to do this or that. We didn't think so. We did it anyway. We were Germans. We didn't even know any English. What were we supposed to talk to each other about, sign language? So as kids we would go up to the school and we'd go behind the barn or wherever, just to speak German. My children didn't learn any English either until they went to school. What do you do to

the innocence of children, you know? I can't help it if they think we're little Hitlers. We were born Americans. But it doesn't mean I can't be proud of who I was or am or whatever. My people had nothing to do with that. We were treated pretty bad but the Japanese were treated even worse. They put them in camps.

I was born about three miles from here on a farm. So was my grandfather, my father and my kids. My brother still owns the home place. I went to school here through the ninth grade. All my kids started school here and in 1964, I believe, this school consolidated with the Fredericksburg Independent School District.

I have spent all my life here, in and around Luckenbach. As far as telling you what it means to be a native Texan, well, that's so hard to explain. I figure, you know, our Maker made us. He put us all in different areas. We don't have a choice about where we're born. We don't get that option. So that's special. I had to have been put here for a certain reason.

I agree that along with the opportunity comes the struggle. This is Texas. Not everything comes easy. I think we're put here to prove that it can be done. Just because times are hard does not mean you're going to survive because it says so in the Good Book. If you try hard enough, you're going to make it. You can't give up.

I think the nicest thing about Texas is the people who live here. The terrain is absolutely gorgeous—most of it. We've got everything, mountains—they may not be magnificent mountains but they're big enough. We have valleys and desert, beautiful lakes, piney woods in East Texas—yeah and eight hundred and somethin' miles from El Paso to Orange, Texas. If you can't find what you need between El Paso to Orange, well, you don't need it.

I was born and raised here. This place means more to me than any other fifteen people put together for the simple reason that it's my home. It's my birthright. I'm a real Luckenbachian—born, raised and papers to prove it. I want to maintain Luckenbach to where it's a family place, where I could take my grandmother or I could take my babies or whatever, and don't have to worry about the F-word or any of that other stuff that's going on out there. I feel like every state needs a Luckenbach, where people can get together right there and have a place to go. It's going to be that way as long as I'm here. I'm not a young chick now. I'm not planning on going anywhere.

Marge Mueller, the Sheriff of Luckenbach, Texas passed away on July 25th, 2004 just weeks after this interview was completed. This may, in fact, have been her last interview. Her ashes were spread throughout Luckenbach. Marge was irrepressible and a true Texan icon. You couldn't miss her long braided hair and rattlesnake earrings. She reflected the character and the unique personality of Luckenbach. Marge once said, "Working in Luckenbach is like taking a trip around the world without all the hassles of traveling. I have bonded with the world." She will always have friends in every corner of the world. Texas has lost one of her finest ambassadors.

STRUGGLE, STRIFE and STRENGTH

CAROL VOIGTEL

★ BIRTHPLACE ★
Dallas, TX
(Home was in Royse City, 30 miles from Dallas)

★ CURRENT RESIDENCE ★
Nacogdoches, TX since 1965

★ OCCUPATION ★
Retired high school counselor

We found Carol at the tourism center in Nacogdoches. She's another example of
someone whose roots are deeply set in Texas. Read closely and you realize
not only her pride, but the deep emotion of belonging to something special.

What is special about Texas? For one thing, the size. Texans didn't very much like it when Alaska became the largest state. That took away part of our bragging rights. Texans are a real proud people. We value our heritage and know it is somewhat different from any other state in the country. After all, we were a Republic before we were a state. We had to win our independence from Mexico, which at that time was the equivalent of the United States winning its independence from England. So I guess that is where part of our pride and tradition came from. I am sure other states may have similar traditions, but we just grew up with the feeling that Texas is special in many different ways.

Some people think Texans are arrogant and braggadocios but I think Texans in general are really optimistic. Things may be going wrong for a while, but still you have that feeling that we are going to come out of this whether its an economic slowdown or whatever, that has affected us as a state. We have optimism and enthusiasm and are very much alive to what is going on in the world. We travel a lot. Texans are big travelers.

One of my favorite traditions in Texas is the Aggies. Aggies are unique. We have five degrees from A&M in our family.

My father's family were sharecroppers. They moved back and forth between Rockwall County and Jack County when he was a little boy. They were trying to improve their lot each time. They were a tough pioneer family.

My great-grandfather, Robert Adam Terrell, on my mother's side, the man that Terrell was named for, was a surveyor. He surveyed when Nacogdoches County came all the way from down here clear to the Red River. He surveyed all of this huge area of Texas as his profession. He was given quite a bit of land around Dallas, which was worthless at the time. There was a gristmill out of Dallas up close to Wiley. He needed a gristmill. He traded land that was close to White Rock Lake in Dallas for a gristmill back at the time when the gristmill was more valuable than the land.

My great grandfather's brother was the Attorney General in Tennessee under

Sam Houston when he was governor there. They came to Texas. His name was Roddock Rockwell George Whitfield Terrell. Then he was Attorney General of Texas under Sam Houston's governorship. So they go back to that generation of Texas.

My grandfather and his two brothers were given adjacent farms from their father's land grant that he had received in payment for his surveys. We had the last of those farms until about four years ago when we sold it. The Terrell heirs had owned that land since the beginning of when it was granted, but we had no use for it up there. That is where my heritage comes from the Terrell side.

I know people have courage everywhere, but I am only familiar with the Texas type of courage. I think Texas got a double dose of it. We have had an awful lot of war heroes come out of Texas, admirals, generals, and presidents. The pride of being born and reared in Texas and of knowing that my family contributed to the building of the state gives the term Native Texas a special meaning. I have a great appreciation for those that came because I can trace my family back to Virginia before the Revolutionary War. I have a great deal of respect for everybody else's heritage, but I am glad that mine came from here.

> I know people have courage everywhere, but I am only familiar with the Texas type of courage.

JOHNNY HENRY

★ BIRTHPLACE ★
Eason, Oklahoma

★ CURRENT RESIDENCE ★
Canyon, TX

★ OCCUPATION ★
Retired Jeweler & Real Estate Agent

We met Johnny in Canyon, Texas at the local Braum's restaurant.

He did not have much to say but what he said got straight to the point.

I have lived in Texas since I was about four years old and I consider myself a Texan. I grew up at Muleshoe and we moved to Canyon in 1972. I lived in San Marcos and Austin for about 12 years. My wife taught school at WT (West Texas State University). But I'm retired now.

I don't know that everybody has the same idea about the history, but it really started with people that weren't from Texas. That's what happened at the Alamo. Most of those people were from out of state or out of country. You don't have to be born here to be a Texan—that is what made the state like it is today. They had to build a state and that made everybody think a little more of us. This was a tough place to make a living and it still is. When people came here, they came to work. I think the work ethic was you always had to work if you wanted anything. We didn't depend on the government.

SARAH GUERRA

★ BIRTHPLACE ★
San Antonio, raised in Sinton, TX

★ CURRENT RESIDENCE ★
Victoria, TX

★ OCCUPATION ★
Retired

*What impressed me so much about Sarah was her spirit. She did not have
it easy growing up. She saw the ugly face of discrimination first hand.
If you were to speak with her, you too would be smitten by her boundless
optimism and how she truly looks for the good in everyone.
It was a privilege to talk with her. She makes a mean dish of enchiladas too.*

What is special to me about Texas is the mixture of the language between Mexico and Texas. It's special to me because I can communicate with the people who are from Mexico and communicate here. Some of my daughters...they understand Spanish but not that much and others do. We've been here all our lives and I believe we see our customers like friends and family. It's more like family. That's the way I feel and my girls feel that way too. I treat all my customers like they were my own family. And that's what makes it so special. I love to talk to them. In my opinion we're supposed to be family. I love Texas—that's what makes it special to me.

As human beings, I believe God created us all equal.
We are supposed to love each other.
God doesn't have color,
He got love for everybody.

We have never been out of Texas, but all the people I have met from all the states, they don't share the same opinion with each other like we do here. Another thing that makes us so special is that we like to treat people like they were our own. Yeah, I'm very proud to be a Texan.

We've seen a lot of change in Texas. For example, when I was a little girl going to school I knew how to read and write Spanish and English. My mother taught me English. My grandfather taught me Spanish. We were going to a country school. We were separated from the white kids. We just had Mexican kids—no blacks—just Mexicans. There were white kids in the high school. They would tell us to bring a pound of hamburger meat, lots of rice, macaroni or whatever. And we would bring it. They would feed us at lunchtime. It would be a mug with beans and two slices of bread. That's what we would get to eat. We couldn't go to the cafeteria and eat with the other kids. Nowadays, all the kids are all together. That's a big improvement.

Growing up was hard. It was hard because, well, for example, we used to ride the bus and the white kids would say, "Oh you Mexican grease. Don't sit by us, stay away from us." When I was growing up I learned to resent people. You weren't allowed to be with white kids until you got to high school—which I never did. I quit the seventh grade so I could get married.

Later when I was married, around '53 or '54, they were leasing some land for oil. My aunt knew some people that had land and they wanted us to go and talk with them. They knew this lawyer from Robstown. He didn't understand Spanish and the people didn't understand English, so they asked me if I could go with them to translate and I said, "Yes." My aunt went with me because she knew the people. We went and they talked to the people about the lease and did business with them.

When we were coming back, somewhere around, I believe, about one o'clock at night, we stopped at this restaurant. We sat down. As other people came in, they were getting served but we weren't. The lawyer got up and went up to the owner and asked, "Why aren't you serving us? We're going to pay." The owner said, right there in

front of us, "We'll serve you and the two little white guys but we don't serve them Mexicans here." The lawyer said, "OK." And so we took off. He told me, "Sarah, this place is going to be closed tomorrow." Me, I was used to that treatment. That's the way it was. Sure enough, when he got to Robstown, he called Corpus (Christi), talked to the LULAC and they closed that place.

There was another restaurant over there in Sinton where we used to live. My husband's father was real light complexioned—he looked like a white man and his eyes were as blue as could be. We would go in and they would give him a cup of coffee in the front. All the Mexican people had to go to the back with the black people to eat when the line was long. There was a big hurt in

us—in me, especially. But then when I started working and mingling with people of all kinds—some blacks, whites and all, I started learning it wasn't the same as it was before.

We had some very special friends when we were growing up. But I'm so glad that it is so different now. We can all eat and live in the same place. We all can talk together.

That love that I didn't get from white people when we were growing up, that probably gave me the courage to love everybody. You know, to be a family. Now we can talk to people, we can go anywhere. Somehow that lets me open up to people. It don't matter what race. To me we're all the same. They all come here (Guerra's Restaurant), blacks, whites, Mexicans and say, "Hi

Grandma!" and they kiss me. That makes me feel like I've accomplished a lot. Whoever walks through that door is my family.

As human beings, I believe God created us all equal. We are supposed to love each other. God doesn't have color, He got love for everybody. I've accomplished a lot. The past is gone—the future is what's important.

Texas covers just over seven percent
of the nation's total area.

JAN TRIPLETT, PH.D.

★ BIRTHPLACE ★
Corpus Christi, TX

★ CURRENT RESIDENCE ★
Austin, TX

★ OCCUPATION ★
Business Coach, COO of a "small business hatchery"

Jan Triplett is a recognized leader and small business advocate in the State of Texas.
She works directly with small business owners and entrepreneurs everyday.
She witnesses this concept of opportunity versus the struggle on a first hand basis.
Here she shares some personal thoughts about Texas and gives
practical advice about dealing with and doing business with Texans.

T exas is special because it is full of itself. It believes it is better and has proof of it. It can point to specific things that make it different. Other people around the country, when you say you are from Texas, whether you're a native or just live here, look at you differently. They have different expectations. When I was ten, my mother and father divorced and we moved to the Midwest. That was during the sixties and that was the beginning of Civil Rights Movement and things of that sort. My fifth grade classmates all looked at me as odd and different. They also assumed that I was a slave trader. Every place I have ever gone and said I was from Texas, I got a different reaction. I grew up in Texas and partially in Illinois. Being from

Chicago didn't have the same resonance with people but people come with an expectation of what a Texan is. What I also got was "you don't sound like a Texan." And since not all of us who are Texans sound like we came from East Texas or West Texas, it is not unusual that I didn't sound like what they considered from the movies.

There were just certain expectations of what I was like, and what I was capable of. I think that many people look at Texans, [and] even though we're a big state, they sometimes lump us all together. The other thing about Texas that I think makes it unique is that it has a sense of history that is separate from the United States. I'm a Texan and I'm an American. Not I am an American who happens to be from Texas. We tend to put that first.

My brother, who lives in Maryland, considers himself a temporary Marylander although he's been there 30 years. He always talks about wanting to come home. What I have found with Texans who are out of state is that they can't wait to get back to wherever in Texas they're from. You never lose that piece of you. That may be true in other states but the people I've met from other places have a sense of home but they didn't have a sense of state. And that to me is very different.

When we went to Japan part of the interest was being from Texas. We had 151

> Texas is special because it is full of itself. It believes it is better and has proof of it.

countries who sent delegations to meet us. And they all wanted to try on my Stetson hat. They all wanted to talk about Texas. They viewed Texas as something different from the United States.

Being a native Texan in some ways gives me a code of conduct. It tells me how I should treat people. It tells me how I should look at the world. People who are from say Finland or Denmark always talk about the high incidence of suicide. Other places dance the tango, which is a very dark dance. Here, we dance the two-step. It's a happy dance. It's a happy movement and it's creative. So part of being a Texan means being a maverick and being able to stand the heat of being one. In certain countries if you are different, you are frowned upon. In Texas, if you're not different, you're frowned upon.

There's an attitude that gets to a sense of self esteem, creativity and wonderment. For example, my nephew got married two years ago and he brought his bride-to-be down here. We went to visit my two uncles. One lived at one end of Texas in Del Rio and the other lived in Pleasanton, south of San Antonio. When you leave Austin and drive to those two cities and back, you've done a fair piece of traveling. The bride to be had never been in Texas. I said to her, "Do you like this feeling of open country?" Because to me, the sky is unlimited. She has always lived in Maryland. She said, "It feels to me as if the sky is falling on me." It's a very different perception of openness.

I think most Texans, and again I think it's also something true of people who come to Texas, have this feeling of expanse and opportunity—that "don't fence me in" mentality. Yes, there are fences but there's a perception that even if things didn't go well, you pick up and move to the next town. You could start all over. You could get a second chance, a third chance, and a fifth chance. There wouldn't be the negativity that could come in smaller communities. Texans embrace that symbolism of falling off a horse and getting right back on.

My friends from Arizona have a different way of looking at that expanse. Certainly they have a number of things in common with Texas, but unless they were farmers and ranchers themselves, they have more of an urban perspective. In Texas, even if we come from urban communities, I think we have more of the rural perspective.

---- ==+== ----

People look to each other for support and that's part of your role as being part of the community. If you are on the road, whether you're male or female, and somebody has stopped—you stop. If somebody wants to pass, you pull over and let them go by. There are just some common things like you wave when you go by and give the thumbs up and a wave to them. There's kind of an extended family.

My oldest friend, whom I've known since I was three, grew up entirely in Corpus [Christi] and is now at Washington and Lee in Virginia. She has always been her own kind of maverick. In Texas at least, even though there was a code of conduct that was similar between male and female, there was still some potentials for women like that pioneer woman who was self sufficient. Yet you might be a pretty little darlin' and need to be taken care of a little bit, but they backed out of your way when you brought your gun out. When a rabid bobcat got in, my stepmother killed it. She was ferocious in terms of protecting her own things. So it's as if there were two sides. There really are differences among Texas women and Texas men and I think some of that is a holdover from that pioneer spirit.

One of the early groups that were here when I came back to school was a group that was beyond consciousness raising. They call themselves "the ladies who lunch." They were behind the scenes kind of women, one of them was Barbara Vacker, who went on to become the head of the Democratic party in Travis county. A lot of those women were doing things that women in other parts of the country were not able to do yet. Women in other places might have been doing it but were not as visible. But Texas women, when they decide to do something, pretty much take the bull by the horns and go forward. They are visionaries. They necessarily don't feel trapped in a lifestyle that they might be uncomfortable with.

When my mother went to girl's school, one of the things she liked to do most was [horseback] riding. She would go ride and she'd have to come back and dress for dinner. And she would have on her boots underneath her formal gown. Even looking at Texas women's roles, they were more creative than perhaps in another part of the country, given the history of the different time periods we're talking about. But also, continuing on, you have a lot of women in the Austin area who have been involved at high levels in terms of technology. They are the new wildcatters.

One thing about Texas, it's either boom or bust. As long as you're willing to live that roller-coaster ride, that's the way it works here. When I was little, we would take the train down from Corpus to Mexico. My brother had asthma. On that train one time was a man from Texas who had a guitar. The trains going down there were strange because you never quite knew whether they would get there on time. There was a drunk porter and he was trying to put people off the train. So there was this guy sitting there strumming his guitar, and he said to the group of us sitting there on the train, "When you ride this train, you've got to stay loose." That's a Texas perspective. You get on this train, you know it's gonna have bumps, and you know it's going to have ups and downs. In Texas, you go to pick up a rock and there is going to be a snake under it or you're going to pick up a rock and oil is gonna gush out from under it. You don't quite

know what's going to happen. We accept that as a fact of life. Instead of fighting it, you simply build that into your expectations. And that means when I look at things that are marketed towards me or when I look at opportunities to buy things, that's the framework in which I make my decisions. Does that fit into my code of ethics? Does it fit into my code of conduct? Does it really stress opportunity? If it's negative or if it doesn't fall into my perspective, I will turn it off.

Texas is a talking state, we will talk to anybody about anything because we hate to wait. Texans will talk to you standing in line. Give them a chance, they will say something. I don't know if it's because of the empty spaces and we're trying to fill it with something but most of this will tell other people how we perceive things. So from a perspective of somebody trying to do business with you in Texas, they need to be aware that the term "networking" might as well have originated in Texas because that's the way we survived—by networking with each other and sharing lots of things. And that's going to be very strong.

Remember, Texas is built on stories. You find lots of people who tell histories. We'll give you a straight answer but there's usually some more stuff.

Because Texas was a harsh land, water has always been an issue. The sun is always an issue and strong weather too. This is a place of extremes. You live each day because you don't know what the next day is going to bring.

Texas is a talking state, we will talk to anybody about anything because we hate to wait.

When you consider the land mass of Texas, it's really kind of amazing. When I was in Illinois, Alaska became the fiftieth state. My classmates delighted in pointing out that Texas was no longer the biggest state. I got so mad. But there is this tremendous sense of pride. I might have been a first generation Texan, it didn't matter. Maybe part of that is because Texas tends to be so full of itself. It resents it when somebody calls that into question.

Texans are friendly. I think when people come from other states, it throws them a bit until they see that there is no expectation or hidden agenda. I just am that way. Texans are much more touchy people, I mean we *touch* people more often. Some of that could be from the Hispanic background. When you know there are long distances and you may not see somebody, you tend to be, I think, more willing to make that human touch.

One of the things I do think is different about Texas is—yes, you can have a second chance. But if you burn me, you do something that not only affects me, but has broader repercussions, then chances are you're not going to get that second chance. Chances are you're going to get run out of state on a rail. Doesn't happen often but if you have improper business dealings or something, Texans simply don't tolerate the bad guys. If they're Robin Hood kind of people that's okay—but if they really hurt somebody, there is a really strong moral outrage that happens. There is a strong sense of protecting the land, the people, animals, whatever. That's a really strong core belief. By protecting each other we, in turn, are protected. We have that expectation. I have this belief, when I do business with you, you will be looking after my best interest. People here are tolerant and they have an expectation. It's like a code of the West or Texas that you sign onto. We just automatically expect that if you're here, you buy into the golden rule.

Texas has always had this entrepreneurial spirit. Texas is third behind California and New York almost every year in terms of how many independent small businesses there are. When down turns come, what you find is instead of people leaving the state to go find other jobs, they tend to stick close to home and start their own business. They have their own support system here. Even if they fail, nobody's going to chastise them very much. Money is not an important issue in Texas. It's about lifestyle and quality of life. We might have to try seven or eight times until we find it, but we're willing to keep at it.

What's so inviting about Texas? I think one of the things is the weather. It can be really hot but it is usually bright and warm. There is a strong thing about if you don't like it here you can go up the road a piece and you'll find something else. There are always alternatives in Texas. In certain states what you see is what you get and that's it.

Texas is a tangible, emotional, visceral reaction. That may be part of the appeal of Texas—there is always this perception that you're going to be surprised.

It behooves people or companies who do business with or in Texas to have a recognition that part of this myth is going to be part of that Texan's psyche. Texans have a grander view of things. They're going to see more possibilities. Texans will just see it bigger than you do.

The dome of the Texas state capitol building in Austin
stands seven feet taller than the U.S. Capitol.
It is also the largest state capitol building in the country.

CLINT LYNCH

★ BIRTHPLACE ★
Dallas, TX—Raised in Waco

★ CURRENT RESIDENCE ★
Austin, TX

★ OCCUPATION ★
Director of Research, Texas State Cemetery

As a history buff, I was engrossed while talking Texas with Clint Lynch.

He really understands what made Texas happen. I came away with

a better understanding of Texas because of this conversation.

To me it's about the history. That's what makes Texas so different. We are basically the only state that was once its own nation. Like the American Revolution, these Texans are transplants who came here and fought for what they believed in. I think that we as Texans have always held that over the heads of the other states. And for the longest time we were the largest state in the Union. Because of that stigma, everything is bigger in Texas. I think that is what makes Texas so special. Look at its history—it's made up of such big personalities that have come here and made Texas what it is today. That is the one thing that really stands out in everybody's mind.

Being here at the cemetery and dealing with all of these people's stories, and dealing with their personal lives, gives you an idea of who these people were. What they had to go through in order to become governor, fight for the Confederacy, or even the fight for

Texas independence. They all overcame such great adversities in their lives. I've always thought Texas was founded in failure. So many of the people who came here—Sam Houston, Jim Bowie, Davy Crockett, William Travis—they all had great adversity in their lives before they moved to Texas. Houston left the governorship of Tennessee. He was a raging alcoholic for seven years of his life. William Travis was caught in a divorce and was in huge debt. Crockett had just lost his reelection campaign for Congress. Bowie came to Texas to avoid being arrested for essentially stealing huge amounts of land in Louisiana. All their lives convened in this one place. Texas offered them the opportunity to start new—start over fresh—make a name for themselves. They all came here and did that.

It wasn't just the big personalities either. So many of the other "small" Texans—we might not know their names—but they came here with Stephen F. Austin's colony or the other different colonies and throughout what eventually became the state. They too were looking for that opportunity. It was the cheap land and the excitement of something new. It goes back to when they left behind poor farms, debt, death, and possible imprisonment. They put the "GTT" on the door. Like a note—Gone To Texas. It represents something new, something that is an opportunity to excel and to do something more than they were able to do in their previous lives.

Texas was a tough place. You still can't tame her. There's just no way. These people not only had to fight the land but the Indians that were there. They had to fight the Mexican government — Spanish government at times—and each other. There was lots of jockeying between the personalities that were living in the colonies. Texas—you can't tame her. Whether it's being a farmer out in West Texas with no water for miles around or trying to catch fish down on the coast, Texas is always going to take care of itself first. The public comes second.

After Texas was founded as a republic, there was no money—just land. That's how they paid their soldiers for fighting. It's how they paid for the capitol. So it's always been about the land. It is still that way today a little. There's the vastness of it as well. When they were trying to figure out how to get Europe to recognize them as an individual nation, it was Anson Jones who realized this was a great cotton area. So

Being here at the cemetery and dealing with all of these people's stories, and dealing with their personal lives, gives you an idea of who these people were.

again, it was the land that helped Texas really kind of grow into what it is today. It made us viable. We're still pulling oil out of the ground, pulling rocks and granite or whatever. We're still raising cattle and growing crops. Even though, with LBJ (Lyndon Johnson) we moved into more of a technological realm, if you drive any of the back roads you're going to drive through farming communities. Texas is still an agricultural state as much as it is anything else.

There has always been the question: is Texas a Southern state or a Western state? I think that if you look at Texas geographically, you could almost draw a line right down the middle and part of it would be a Southern state and the other part Western. They're totally different like the advertising terms "It's like a whole other country" or something like that. You've got the desert, the mountains of West Texas, the Piney Woods and the coast of East Texas. It just blows people's minds that you can still be in the same place but have so many differences. I just don't think people can understand Texas and its diversity until they come here and are able to experience it.

The Alamo gives you chills when you walk into it. You're in a true Texas shrine. A hundred eighty some odd people lost their lives in there. The image of Davy Crockett on top of the wall swinging "Old Betsy"—that's the reality of what happened. It was hand-to-hand. They were completely out of ammunition with thousands of Mexican soldiers streaming over the walls. There was nothing else they could do.

I have always loved what I call the romantic ideals of history. You know,

Crockett swinging that gun or Albert Sydney Johnston, the Confederate General that's buried out here. He had already been wounded once in a duel back here in Texas and as a result, he had no feeling in his right leg. He led this group of Tennessee militiamen into battle at Shiloh. Lo and behold, he gets shot in back of that right knee. Yet, you see the general on his white horse with the great name "Fire Eater" with his sword in the air leading the charge. It's that romantic ideal of history that attracts so many people. I think it's the romantic ideal of the Alamo or the Battle of San Jacinto of the little guy coming up to the big guy. And you may not win the battle, but you can dang sure win the war. Here we were, both times, grossly outnumbered. We did more damage to them both times than they did to us. That is such a huge draw to people. That's why the Alamo has millions of visitors a year.

Being a native Texan makes me feel special. It kind of sets you apart from everybody else. We've got bigger personalities, we drive bigger trucks with bigger tires on them, bigger Cadillacs, whatever. You're just a part of something bigger. Texas is just so much bigger than we are. That may sound stupid but there is so much here. That may be why so many people vacation here and want to come here or want to move here.

I love my job more than anything because I get to share with anybody who walks through here. My co-workers make fun of me because I sometimes stop people on the grounds and ask them if they need any help and we'll start talking and telling stories. I get to know and learn all this information and it's my job to tell people about it or to write about it. The Texas State Cemetery is the only one of its kind anywhere in the United States—a cemetery specifically run by the state for its public officials and heroes. No other state does that.

It goes back to Texas taking care of its own—making sure that its history is right out there in front. It may sound a little crass but you can go out here and see an entire collection of Texas public officials, heroes, and Civil War Generals. I think that is why the cemetery is the only one of its kind. We have everything out here.

In school, Texas history is taught in fourth grade and seventh and when you catch them so young, it gives them a sense of being Texan. Whether you had an ancestor that fought at the Alamo or you were born 25 years later, that's a part of you and your history. You're the Texan. You may not be related to Sam Houston but you know his story. You know about him getting shot at San Jacinto and his being deposed as the governor of the state of Texas. That's part of who you are—the good, bad and the ugly. Again, I think that is what pushes the Texans because we are backed by so much. We got that swagger. We can drive those big trucks and those big Cadillacs and have oil wells and ride horses.

We're also the only ones who can fly their flags at the same height as the U.S.

flag. We traded three million acres of land to pay for the Capitol. It is that glamorization that pushes Texas to the forefront. You know, the big tall Texan—like Big Tex up at the State Fair. It just radiates. People are drawn to it because nobody else has what we have here.

We once had an exhibit in the gallery and we had two pairs of governor's cowboy boots. One was a pair of Governor George Bush's and one from Governor Ann Richards. Governor Richards' boots were red, white and blue with a star on one side and the yellow rose on the other. Governor Bush's had the state seal sown into them. You see it in clothing everywhere. There is a gentleman traveling around the state with pictures of just the word Texas and he's put it in a poster and he's doing another one of our state symbol the star. He's gone to all the counties and everywhere he sees it.

We push our image so much, it's like we want everyone to be a Texan. We kind of feel sorry for everybody else. Texas is so hard to talk about sometimes because there are so many different aspects of it. You can be in Nacogdoches or even further north and feel like you're somewhere else—just listen to the different accents that we have. You can always read more about Texas but you will never know everything.

Just about every one here on the grounds of the Texas State Cemetery came from somewhere else. We had signers who came from New York, England, and Ireland. If you were to walk through the Confederate fields, you'll find a guy born in Prussia buried here—and England, France and Italy. It's amazing how all their histories converged in Texas. They may happen to be buried next to each other and they never knew each other but what they had in common was Texas.

The San Jacinto Monument near Houston
is one of the tallest columns in the world. At 570 feet,
it's about twenty feet higher than the Washington Monument.

Texas has 254 counties, the most of any state in the country.

Of the nation's ten largest cities, three are in Texas
(Houston, Dallas, and San Antonio).

15 percent of the population lives in rural Texas.

196 of the 254 counties are classified as rural.

Rhode Island would fit into Texas 220 times.
41 counties in Texas are larger than Rhode Island.

Approximately 97 percent of Texas is privately owned land.

What follows is a story I wrote about the Texas State Cemetery for the

July 2002 issue of CountryLine Magazine. It is without a doubt, one of my favorite places

in the entire state. There is more Texas history buried out there than you can imagine.

I find it inspiring. I first visited for a memorial ceremony on Texas Independence Day

that year. The Texas re-enactors were there and fired muskets and cannons to

commemorate the lives of those who fought for Texas Independence.

It was impressive and had a lasting affect on me. No trip to Austin would be complete

for any devoted Texan without an hour or two at this hallowed place.

Browse the grounds and you will begin to understand what Texans are about

and why they feel the way they do about Texas.

Texas State Cemetery

It is that time of year when our thoughts reflect upon our nation's colorful history. We remember the Declaration of Independence, the minutemen and patriots past. We recall the courage and sacrifices of these men and women who paid the ultimate price for the privilege of freedom that we take for granted today. Texas too, has its share of heroes; people whose sacrifice was as big and as important as anyone who has ever loved their country.

There is a remarkable place about four blocks east of Interstate 35 in downtown Austin where native Texans and tourists can, arguably, find more Texas history than anywhere in the state. The Texas State Cemetery is the final resting place of some of the most famous people Texas has ever produced. If you have

any interest in Texas history at all—this is a must see.

Buried in the cemetery are the remains of eleven Texas Governors, five Lieutenant Governors, five Speakers of the Texas House of Representatives, fourteen Signers of the Texas Declaration of Independence, three U.S. Senators from Texas, four U.S. House of Representatives from Texas, four Texas First Ladies, four authors, 31 Texas Rangers, another ten Republic of Texas Veterans, nine Confederate Generals, two Texas patriots who actually fought in the American Revolution before coming to Texas, and one Congressional Medal of Honor recipient. You will also find the graves of 1,811 Confederate soldiers and 350 of their wives.

The first person to be buried there was Edward Burleson. Along with Ben Milam, he was instrumental in the original siege at Bexar in 1835. As General of the Texas Army, he led the largest number of troops at the Battle of San Jacinto. He became the Vice-President of the Republic of Texas and founder of its capitol, Waterloo—later to be renamed—Austin. He also started the first cotton gin in San Marcos. He died in Austin in 1851. A committee was quickly formed and one of its members, Andrew Jackson Hamilton provided his personal property of eighteen acres for a place to bury the Texas hero, but the state did not take possession of the land until 1854. Burleson remained the only person in the cemetery until 1856, when Abner S. Lipscomb, an Associate

Justice of the Texas Supreme Court, was interred. Over the next ten years both veterans of Texas' fight for independence and Civil War generals were buried there.

It was the Civil War, resulting in the death of several Texas officers who were killed that peaked the interest in the state cemetery. A year after the Civil War, an acre was put aside for Union soldiers, but in 1880 those remains were removed. Most of them now rest in the national cemetery in San Antonio. There is one Union soldier on a hill by himself. He served under Brigadier General Edmund J. Davis in the 1st Texas Cavalry—the only Union outfit formed in Texas during the Civil War. He was originally buried in Oakwood Cemetery in Austin but later the Cemetery Committee and his family agreed he should reside in an area known as Federal Point in the far northeast corner. Today you can find his headstone perched on the hilltop. It is the resting place of Antonio Briones, Civil War Veteran, 1844-1938.

The most distinctive and elaborate monument in the cemetery belongs to Civil War General Albert Sydney Johnston. One of many of Texas' colorful characters, he served as a Commander of the Army and Commander of the Western Forces. At one point in his life, he was wounded in a duel and although he recovered from his wounds, he suffered a partial paralysis and loss of feeling in his leg. During the Battle of Shiloh he was shot behind the knee, but despite his injury, he continued to lead his troops. Unfortunately, the wound was more severe than he realized and he bled to death. Johnston, originally buried in New Orleans, was moved to the Texas property in 1867. Thirty-five years later, Elizabeth Ney, a famous artist of the day, was commissioned to design a fitting monument for the fallen general. She sculpted a life size death mask of white marble that was placed in a chapel-like structure easily visible from Seventh Street.

In the later years of the nineteenth century, the State of Texas assumed control of the Confederate Veteran's Home in Austin. As the soldiers began to die, it was decided they should be buried with the Confederate generals. In 1871 the legislature authorized the state to provide a headstone with each one's name, date of birth and death and the name of the unit they served. The headstone cost was not to exceed $40. In most Christian cemeteries the headstones face the east, but in the Texas State Cemetery, the Confederate headstones face the west. There is not a definitive answer why this is the case. The last Confederate to die in Texas was in 1954 at 108 years old.

Perhaps the most famous resident of the cemetery is Stephen F. Austin, the "Father of Texas," who brought the first 300 settlers to Texas. Upon his death from pneumonia in 1836, Austin was buried in Peach Point in Brazoria County. At the request of Governor Oscar B. Colquitt, Austin was brought to the State Cemetery in 1910. Pompeo Coppini sculpted the bronze likeness of the Texas icon that sits upon the monument today. At one point, the statue was supposed to sit at the south end of the Congress Street Bridge and point toward the Capitol, but for whatever reason that idea was never pursued and it was moved onto the monument you see today.

Pompeo Coppini created several sculptures for the University of Texas that you can see around the Austin campus. Another one of Coppini's striking works is the memorial for Joanna Troutman who designed and created the first Texas flag. The flag bore a five point blue star on white fabric with the words "Liberty or Death." James Fannin raised the flag over Goliad when told of the signing of the Texas Declaration of Independence. The irony is that Troutman never set foot in Texas in her life. She was from Georgia. Still, Gov. Colquitt re-interred Troutman in the cemetery in 1913 for her contribution to Texas.

There are so many Texas notables to find on the grounds that you cannot help but become inspired and humbled at the same time. Here you will find Texas Ranger, "Big Foot" Wallace, arguably one of the toughest rangers to have ever lived. Wallace led a colorful life. He ran the mail between San Antonio and El Paso—some of the most dangerous country on the continent at that time. He was involved in the infamous Black Bean Affair, and he is reported to be a descendant of the family of Scottish freedom fighter William Wallace of "Braveheart" fame.

Ma and Pa Ferguson, both two-time governors, share an intricately carved monument. Authors include J. Frank Dobie, Texas folklore writer and recipient of the "Medal of Freedom" awarded by President Lyndon Johnson. Fred Gipson, the author of the classic book, *Old Yeller* rests here as well. James Logan is the only Congressional Medal of Honor recipient buried there. He's near the monument honoring all Texas recipients of the Medal of Honor. A little known fact that I learned by reading the names on the stone is that the medal was also awarded for actions in the Indian wars.

The first of the eleven governors to be laid to rest there was, perhaps, the most unpopular leader the state ever had. Edmund J. Davis rests under the tallest monument—some 30 feet from base to top. He was a Republican governor in 1870 when the Reconstruction Era was hard on Texas. Interestingly enough, during the Civil War, Davis had been ordered by Abraham Lincoln to form the 1st Texas Calvary, which is the same outfit Antonio Briones served. Popularity was not something the Reconstuctionist governor ever had to be concerned about. When he narrowly lost the next election to a Democrat, he refused to leave office and was physically removed from the Governor's office. His brother was a well to do businessman who owned Key Biscayne in Florida. He had the large obelisk placed over the grave.

John Connolly's memorial is particularly striking. It is black marble with a white marble statue of Saint Andrew that once adorned Westminster Abbey in the 1500s. When the Protestants became the dominant religion in England, some of the saints fell out of favor and their likenesses were removed. This particular statue moved around Europe over the centuries until Mrs. Connally, while in Spain, purchased it. After the former governor died, the statue was incorporated into the monument designed by the governor's widow.

As if Texas history is not colorful enough, there are two soldiers in the state cemetery who actually fought in the American Revolution. Robert Rankin and Stephen Williams both fought in the American Revolution, the War of 1812, then traveled to Texas and participated in the Texas Revolution. Word has it that these guys just loved to fight.

Barbara Jordan, the first African-American to be elected to the Texas Senate and the first African-American woman to go to the U.S. Congress from The South, rests in a space on Republic Hill. She was a wonderful speaker and came to national prominence during the Watergate hearings in the 1970s.

Another person who was important to the development of the cemetery was Louis Kemp. As the centennial celebration approached, Kemp was responsible for having 76 famous Texans brought here for reburial. In fact, the shortest highway in the state is Highway 165 and is named for him. It runs through the middle of the 18 acres of the Texas State Cemetery.

No story about the cemetery should be told without mentioning the contributions of Bob Bullock. His love for Texas was so deep that he took on the renovation of the cemetery as his personal project. The work began in 1994. Bullock was known to visit the cemetery at night to be near the people interred there who inspired him. They finally gave him his own key so he wouldn't have to jump the fence in the dark.

As part of the restoration, all the confederate headstones were taken down and cleaned or replaced. Wholesale landscaping was undertaken including the installation of a visitor's center and gallery, a pond, the columbarium wall and a memorial plaza. The cost of the project approached 5 million dollars. By 1997, the work was completed and was dedicated by then Governor George W. Bush with a very proud Bob Bullock by his side. The grounds are meticulously taken care of by the cemetery's superintendent, Harry Bradley. When asked about this hallowed place he stated, "I do feel responsible. I used to worry about doing everything right." It is the only state supported cemetery in the country. According to Bradley, "The most important responsibility is conducting funerals as they are needed." They also do research on the people who are buried there. The operation is watched over by a committee of three appointed by the governor. Currently, they are Martin L. Allday, Chairman, George Christian and Ralph Wayne.

If you're thinking you'd like to be buried along side some these Texans luminaries, hold on. There is only three ways to meet the requirements. First you must be a member or ex-member of the Texas Legislature or an elected state official or appointed and confirmed by the Legislature, designated by governor's proclamation. Also, the cemetery committee can select a person, as well as a place for the spouse for anyone meeting those conditions.

With shade from the canopy of trees overhead, you can meander at your own pace to read the headstones, inscriptions and memorials of these Texas patriots. It is a moving experience. These were once living breathing people who lived lives that made a difference for all of us who love Texas.

There are just too many stories to tell, surpassed only by the myths that have grown up as well. This historical place is packed with Texas history. The cemetery is approximately half full. It is open 365 days a year, 8 a.m. to 5 p.m. It's located at 909 Navasota Street, just off Seventh Street. Admission is free and tours are available. Approximately 10,000 people tour the grounds each year. If you would like to find out more, you can reach their website at www.cemetery.state.tx.us.

This is a truly fascinating and inspiring place. If you have a love for Texas history, your time in Austin is not complete until you have spent some time at this Texas shrine. The Texas State Cemetery is to Texas what Arlington is to the nation. Take the time to visit and you will come away with a new appreciation for this place you call home.

MS. ANONYMOUS

★ BIRTHPLACE ★
Pecos, TX

★ CURRENT RESIDENCE ★
Pecos, TX

★ OCCUPATION ★
Retired Rancher/Farmer

~ *Ms. Anonymous, whose name is not important, is the real deal.*
For the most part, she has been a life long resident of far West Texas.
This lady is the living definition of pioneer stock. Her words reflect
the passion and the strength of her convictions. This lady exudes the character
of many people who live there. She spoke frankly during our visit, like a
typical Texan (if there is such a thing) and she didn't pull punches. ~

hen you stop and think about the people who came here and did things, it wasn't easy. It wasn't easy at all. Anything in this country has not been easy. I can tell you first hand.

My parents came here just exactly a hundred years ago. They got off the train in Monahans, Texas. The icicles were hangin' from the water tower clear to the ground. They stayed in a little frame hotel called the Holman Hotel. Their family came out here to start over and build and do. They had a son. His name was Gene Holman. He became president of Standard Oil. Imagine that. A lot of people have made their fortunes out here and took their money and left because it was too hard to live. You had to carry water in a bucket. I'm still carrying water in a bucket up at one of the ranches. It's still pretty primitive in spots—pretty western.

I'm one of the few native Pecos, Texans still living here. I was born here. Except for my growing up years when I was going to school and during WWII, I've lived in Pecos or in the surrounding areas.

Texas is special because it was hard and you had to work to get here and you had to work to stay here. Everything about it is different. A lady I once knew told me, "I've done everything from build fence to run a whorehouse and there ain't no easy way to make a living in West Texas." She actually said that, and that was true. She did it. She was a great gal.

Nothin' is easy. One year in about 1956, we had about eleven farms all the way from Grand Falls, Barstow; clear down to the Rio Grande and Balmorreah. On October the 26th, we had 13 hails [hail storms] when we were starting to pick. That didn't count the year we had a flood in Presidio. You see that's hard when you've borrowed a million dollars to grow crops and you have to pay the million dollars back plus interest. It ain't easy.

Texas is about the land. You make your livin' off the land. That's what's wrong with Pecos right now. It's gone down

Being a native Texan comes from within.

hill. We don't have anything and the buildings are boarded up because Pecos has lived off of farming and ranching, oil exploration—anything that we had came from the soil. We have wonderful water. In the late 1950s and through the '60s, we had vast farms, 50,000 acres of cotton and it was irrigated with these deep wells with Caterpillar engines—lifting the water like 400 to 550 feet. Good water—could irrigate—the government came in and took our labor away from us.

Suddenly, you don't have any labor, anybody to irrigate for you and you have a section of land out there. What are you going to do? So they started in trying to pick the cotton with the mechanical pickers. They're pretty good now, but costs just as much to irrigate that expensive cotton as it does that short staple cotton and you don't get the difference. So you go out of business. The bankers take a beatin'. If you can pay 'em, you pay 'em. If not, they take your land.

Go look at all those farms that should be farming right now. We don't have any labor. You cannot pay $5.15 an hour for stoop labor. It's all about water and labor. Now instead of 32 cents a thousand for your gas that ran those big Caterpillar pumps, you know what the price of natural gas is now? The price of cotton stays what it was so you can't operate like that. You can't raise vegetables because you have to have water. Now the people from over in Midland want to come over and buy the water right out from under the land. So really we just have nothing but a dust bowl. See it isn't easy. If you stay, well, I guess I'm cynical. I accept it. I stay here. I've had a good life. City life really doesn't appeal to me. I've been there.

Being a native Texan comes from within. You're just proud of yourself because you do the right thing. Sure we have a bunch of crooks and criminals, liars and cheaters but you have to stand up to them. Stand up and be counted. That's what I believe in.

There were twelve of us, three sisters, eight brothers and we grew up together. As a family, we weren't rich but we had adequate everything. We got up in the morning. The first thing was make your bed, and you dress and come in and we all had breakfast together. That's how we started our day. Everyone packed their lunches and went off to work or school. That evening we'd all come back and have dinner together. I thought about that many times because that molded me, not that we were perfect, but it helped us to become who we are. My father was a building contractor. He built the first road up to McDonald Observatory. During the Depression we didn't have any money to spend or throw around but we had plenty of food, and good clothes, and a roof over our head. We all stayed together. We made mistakes. I'll tell you how I looked at it. It helped us to build ourselves, each person. There was some pretty stiff discipline. If you acted up at the table, you got sent out. You learned manners. I thought everyone was doing that.

Here's the thing. We had a garden. In those days, the grocery stores didn't have fresh vegetables. When my mother came to West Texas in 1904, she brought seed from her grandmother's garden. She always had a garden and at least two milk cows. We had animals; we all took care of things. We all had chores and I think those were the kind of things that helped me to become the person I am. We learned responsibility at an early age. We weren't given anything. During the Depression my sister and I, we made twenty-five cents a week if we did all our chores. Out of the twenty-five cents, we gave ten cents to the Sunday school every Sunday. We had ten cents to go to the movies and five cents for a sack of popcorn, if we were careful. So you learned how to take care of your money. I had some milk goats and I milked them and I'd sell the milk to people with children who couldn't tolerate cow's milk for 18 cents a quart. Now you can go buy a quart of goat's milk and it'll cost you about four dollars. Those were the things we were responsible for. We had to do our part.

Texas has been an adventure. When the people came to develop the oil and gas, it was a great adventure. When they hit it, they were successful. When they didn't hit it, they pulled up stakes and moved on. There were all the people who came to develop those farms all around Pecos. It was great. It was a marvelous thing. You almost couldn't believe it.

When the United States had a Bracero Program, that was when we could contract men from Mexico to come and work the farms, we had the Trans-Pecos Cotton Association. Each area had these work associations and you could go and make application if you had one section of land or half a section or and acre—whatever you needed and you paid to get those men transported. They came to the border by the thousands. It was the best good neighbor policy we ever had.

The contracted men were brought up here in buses, wagons or trucks, whatever. They were brought to the associations and the farmers would put in their order. They would make a contract with those workers and take them out to the farms. We had to have good housing, good everything for them—showers, cook shacks, the whole deal. And it worked. It was about ten years when the contract was up. (For questionable, murky political reasons, it was never renewed.) That was the beginning of the labor problems.

For the past 15 years, we've had no rain. You talk about drought. There's nothing sticking up here but Ochoa cactus. You have to have a lot of spirit or else you wouldn't be here.

The W. T. Waggoner Estate Ranch is located
13 miles south of Vernon, TX. The ranch consists
of approximately 520,000 acres. It is recognized
as the largest ranch in Texas surrounded by one fence.

THE BIG "D"...
DIVERSITY

DICK VOIGTEL

★ BIRTHPLACE ★
Corvallis, OR

★ CURRENT RESIDENCE ★
Nacogdoches, TX

★ OCCUPATION ★
Retired Professor of Stephen F. Austin State University

It's obvious this man has taken the time to think about Texas.

He touches on some of the several levels Texans must envision when

they reflect upon Texas. He starts by talking about why it is special.

I think it's the diversity. Texas can offer almost anything somebody wants if they are reasonable about it. We have the wide-open spaces. We have the timbered part of the state. We have the mountains of far West Texas—the Guadalupe area. We have the beaches. We have great geographical diversity as well as cultural diversity.

As far as the people go, the people have come to Texas from so many different origins. That also helps to enhance the color and the beauty of the culture itself. There are more and more native-born Texans, but when you get to our generation there are a lot of people who have been brought here by chance from other areas and each of us has brought the culture that created us. We live our own situation, but we put our own interpretation on it. I think that's one reason that this is an exciting state to live in. For some people, it can be a frustrating state to live in. It just depends on how they interpret their challenges.

In some areas the Mexican cultures are trying to take it back and by population they are growing in great numbers. We have some dear friends in Corpus. They tell us they can see the gradual transition, there is more and more Hispanic influence down in that part of South Texas. It's not bad, it's just different.

There is an attitude here. Some of it is hype and I think it is overly exaggerated from people in other areas. For example, I think President Bush is getting a bum rap from a lot of the Northeastern press because they're trying to portray him in ways that he really isn't. And because people can't identify with that, their first defense sometimes is to play it down or minimize it. I feel like that has burdened him to a certain extent. A lot of Texans, because of how they are being perceived by others, are not fully understood and appreciated because, somehow, we're supposedly bigger than life and somewhat braggartly about it, and yet I don't see it that way because I'm not like that. I feel like we have wonderful people in Texas like we have in any other state in the Union.

Here in Nacogdoches we still revel in the fact that Texas was once its own country. So much of Nacogdoches can be directly traced to the time before Texas even became a republic—when we were still part of Mexico.

A lot of the future leadership of Texas came from the United States. The Sabine River was the international boundary. A lot of people from Tennessee, Alabama, Mississippi, Georgia, and Virginia were all moving this way. When land was available from the Mexican government, they migrated westward to take advantage of these growth opportunities. A lot of these people were very strong in their home states. For example, Sam Houston was the governor of Tennessee before he came to Texas. Of course, he became our first governor as well. Nacogdoches was the port of entry to Mexico. A lot of people passed through here and an a lot of them stayed and left their indelible mark.

Texas was not for the faint of heart. There was a lot of disease here in those days because there was a lot of moisture. There were a lot of swamps, a lot of mosquitoes and disease. These were hard times. It was a lot harder trying to create something in a heavily wooded area than it is in the plains area where you don't have as much vegetation to conquer.

I'm proud to be a Texan. I'm a product of circumstances—the federal government assigned my parents here—my dad was a federal government employee back when World War II started. This has been my life. Texas has been very good to my family and to me. All of our four children still live in various parts of Texas. I married a native Texan and I feel very comfortable, but very humble too. I don't know what my life would have been had I been anywhere else. A lot of the opportunities and challenges the state has given me have made me a better contributing citizen. I have appreciated that opportunity.

CLAUDE PHILLIPS

★ BIRTHPLACE ★
Winters, TX

★ CURRENT RESIDENCE ★
Canyon, TX

★ OCCUPATION ★
Retired Oil Field Worker

He totally gets the concept of several states within Texas.
He was the first to verbalize the political separations around the state.
He's not sure why but he does know they exist. Trying to explain why the liberals
are where they are versus why the conservatives are where they are
is something that needs to be undertaken at another time.

ne thing I want to comment on is people's idea of Texas. Many think it's all alike, but there are absolutely distinct areas. The people are just as much different in one area as any other in the state. The western part of the state from say Midland on west is different from Abilene or Fort Worth then on east. It's like there's states within the state. I've often wondered about that—why it is that way.

Texans are not only different from people in other states but they're different from each other. The Panhandle, politically, is real conservative. I guess Dallas is to a certain extent. But then The South tends to be more liberal. I don't understand why it's that way. East Texas is a lot more liberal than we are out west and in The Panhandle area.

As far as The Panhandle goes—the people and the weather—I like 'em both. Amarillo is big enough to have most of the things you need. We don't have the heavy traffic to contend with. Sometimes you may have to drive 50 miles to go have a steak but 50 miles up here is no big deal.

I really don't know what it means to be a native Texan. I can't find a description for it. You're just born that way. That's the only thing I can tell ya. You do just about anything you're big enough to do.

The hamburger was invented in Athens, Texas by "Ole Dave" Fletch Davis in1904. However, a strong case exists for an Okie serving the first hamburger on a bun in Tulsa as early as 1891. I'm content to let others argue the point. Frankly, as long as cows have been around, I find it hard to believe it took that long for someone to figure out how to make a hamburger.

OLIN MURRELL

★ BIRTHPLACE ★
Gainesville, TX

★ CURRENT RESIDENCE ★
Nashville, TN

★ OCCUPATION ★
Professional Songwriter, Entertainer

Olin is a songwriter in Nashville, Tennessee. He's been writing songs forever.
We worked a radio talk show together in Austin back in the late '80s.
That's when I learned he was born up in North Texas.
He's smart, well read and knows a thing or two about Texas.

I t's one of the state of mind kind of things, Texans sort of believe their own BS. And it's pretty good BS. If I had to think of two words to describe Texas, it would be *gentle steel*. You've seen these big old hairy Texas cow men—sixty years old, their faces look like a roadmap and they've got a hat that weighs 40 pounds on their head. They have a pocket knife that would be illegal in seven states and they can pick up a little baby calf and kiss it right on the nose. And then they can turn right around and put a piece of hot iron on that little calf's butt to make sure that everybody knows it's theirs. They treat people the same way. They can be as hard as nails or they can be as gentle as a lamb. And it all comes out of the same psyche. If you were to ask me where that comes from, I have no earthly idea. I suspect it's the last remaining vestige of the pioneer spirit. I live in Tennessee now and I find they

Texas pride, that whole attitude comes from the pioneer spirit and the unique ability Texans have to believe their own BS. Texas can make fun of itself as much as it brags on itself.

are much the same way. There is a whole lot of similarity between Tennessee and Texas. Even some of the laws seem to track one another.

Texas, as you well know, was built mostly by neer-do-wells, miscreants, out right outlaws and folks on the lam from their wives. They came from everywhere—West Virginia, Virginia, Tennessee, Georgia. Texas was basically a state that was sort of like a penal colony. It was a place people ran to get away from something or somebody. It was a land of second chances and it remains that. You can still get second chances all over Texas. People are always willing to cut you a little bit of slack if you show them you've got the sand to make something out of yourself.

If you've got to live on the land in Texas, you'll earn everything you get. Even in the eastern part of Texas where you get sufficient rainfall to actually grow a few crops and actually fatten up some cows or grow whatever livestock that floats your boat, it is rough scrabble. The farther west you go, the rougher it gets. I used to play a house concert out in Midland. The big joke out there then was that there weren't any trees. I said that I don't wanna hear again that there

aren't any trees in West Texas. I passed it on my way here. The tree was in a place called Garden City, the most inappropriately named town in North America. It had one tree, fourteen trailer parks, two run down buildings, and a service station. It was hardly a wide spot in the road. I'm sure if you stopped, those people would be just as proud as punch about it. They had a tree.

———

Now this is going to sound harsh—maybe it is, maybe it isn't—and it's partly true and partly not true, but it's only been in the last 20 or 30 years that Texans have really started to learn how to take care of the land. I grew up on a small farm in north central Texas just below Oklahoma. I used to say I was four miles from being an Okie. In Oklahoma, they knew about terracing and crop rotation, they knew about all the things that historically people have done to preserve land and its "growability". But in West Texas, where you have very little rain, when cotton started making its march, cotton was a great waster of land. If you look at the East Coast—from the savannas of Georgia—and watch how cotton marched westward, you'll see years and years of crop failure behind it. Cotton just absolutely sucks every nutrient out of the soil. The cotton farmers would grow cotton until the land would no longer generate money-making crops. Then they moved westward.

The Oklahoma aquifer, which is most of the Panhandle and most of West Texas down toward the Permian Basin, is one of the largest aquifers in North America and goes up nearly to Canada. It's huge. In West Texas they took the water table that was at 100 feet and stretched it to 400 feet. That's how much water they sucked out of the ground—just to grow crops. It's only been the last 30 years that they've tried to take care of some of that stuff. At least they were big enough to understand they had made a mistake, learned how to correct it and then took the steps to do it.

In some ways the lower Rio Grande Valley has not changed since 1836, except they have cars and electricity. It's an area that defines struggle. Look up the word struggle in the dictionary and you'll find a picture of Marfa or Balmorreah or any of those little towns down there. It's a constant fight against the elements, the land, and each other. Another thing, the Mexicans had to fight the Rangers. A lot of them were born in Texas. There are some seventh, eighth and ninth generation Mexicans born in Austin or San Antonio who are still looked down on in some circles.

People just do not understand or comprehend the size of Texas. In fact, if you go from Brownsville, the very bottom tip of Texas, to the very top of the Panhandle, you would have driven right at 1,100 miles. That is roughly half the distance to Canada. Texas covers a major chunk of the Central Time Zone and its westernmost city, El Paso, is in the Mountain Time zone.

Texas pride, that whole attitude comes from the pioneer spirit and the unique ability Texans have to believe their own BS. Texas can make fun of itself as much as it brags on itself. That's a unique balance I think. I think that has a lot to do with the attitude. We can make fun of us, we can brag about us.

CURTIS GRAVES

★ BIRTHPLACE ★
New Orleans, Louisiana

★ CURRENT RESIDENCE ★
Tucker, Georgia

★ OCCUPATION ★
Retired Texas State Legislator, Civil Rights Activist, NASA Educator

~ ~

In March of 1960, Curtis Graves was one of fourteen students to participate
in the first sit-in west of the Mississippi River at Weingarten's near the Houston
TSU campus. After graduation, Curtis worked at Standard Savings and Loan in the heart of
the black district, Ward 5, in Houston. It was during this period he decided
to run for political office. Curtis Graves was the first black state representative
to serve in the State House since Texas Reconstruction.

I came to Texas to attend Texas Southern University in 1959. I had completed my second year at Xavier University. I wanted to get out of the house and move away from home. I got my transcript from Xavier sealed. I drove to Baton Rouge in my '51 Mercury to talk to a friend of mine who was the head of the Political Science Department at Southern University. My studies had been in math. I wanted to change fields because I couldn't see myself doing anything in mathematics. I said I wanted to go into Business Administration. The two black schools he recommended were Texas Southern and Tennessee State. I asked, "Which one is the closest?" This is two days before Labor Day. You registered the day after Labor Day. Texas Southern was the closest. He picked up the phone and called the Registrar, a friend, and gave a recommendation. I drove to Houston. That's how I got to Texas Southern and I built a career on that.

What makes Texas special? You've got a collection of chest beaters and yahoos and rugged individualists who cannot take "no" for an answer. You put that combination together in a gumbo and you've got yourself something else. It is a different place. Take my friend John Eslinger. He is a perfect example of Texas. Through sheer ingenuity and drive he has re-invented himself four or five times, and every time he comes out on top. That is the prototypical Texan. He's a midget who has reinvented himself four or five times and he stands tall. He's this little guy who is

> Texas is kind of the last frontier where people, through sheer determination, will decide to do something and it will happen.

going to make it no matter what. He's an absolutely fascinating guy.

Texas is kind of the last frontier—and maybe Alaska—where people through sheer determination will decide to do something and it will happen. T. Boone Pickens and those kinds of guys, they just make it happen.

I do know there is something individual and unique about the Texas mentality. I remember when I first thought about running for the Texas legislature and I was talking to a man in Houston. I told him I was from Louisiana and I didn't know if I could make it here. He said, "Jesus didn't make it in Nazareth either." That was his answer. I said "Oh, you know, you're right." I had been involved in Texas. People knew me. I had gotten arrested in Texas. Because I had developed a Texas legacy, the fact that I had originally come from Louisiana didn't matter.

The King Ranch is larger than the state of Rhode Island.

LARRY HOWARD

★ BIRTHPLACE ★
Merkel, TX

★ CURRENT RESIDENCE ★
San Angelo, TX

★ OCCUPATION ★
Pastor, San Angelo United Methodist Church, San Angelo, TX

Larry Howard has seen various segments of life as it was lived in West Texas.
He is now the Pastor of the First United Methodist Church in San Angelo.
This conversation, however, was held in the library of the Manchaca United
Methodist Church in Manchaca, Texas—a small community just south of Austin—
when he was the pastor of that church. I found his answers to be particularly thoughtful.
When Reverend Howard was told that 70 percent of the population of Texas
resides within 200 miles of Austin, he was surprised and commented,
"I'd bet the other 30 percent are glad of that!"

There is a special Texas identity that people who live here have or soon develop. Why is there that identity? There are many answers to that question, I suspect that my answer would be Texas pride. Some will say it's because we're big. I think it's because we're willing to lay claim to being Texans, whatever that is. People are willing to have that as an identity. My wife is from the Midwest, born and reared in Ohio, and I don't sense the same desire or willingness on the part of people who live in Ohio to say that "I am an Ohioan"—whatever that is. Whereas, the people of Texas are willing to do that. I think that at some point somebody established a particular Texas identity. It might be because of our history as a nation for nine years before we became a state, but that identity was established and has continued to be communicated, and received, and believed because some find value in that identity as a Texan.

I'm in the mystery and mythical business so I find the importance of myth and mystery to be great; even when it's not always true and historically verifiable. So I think there are myths about Texas—that we're rugged, self reliant and decisive. And I think those myths will have proven to be true at times and shown not to be completely true at times, but we see ourselves that way. That's the vision we hold before ourselves as Texans. Whether it's Lyndon Johnson or George W. Bush, I think they want to see themselves as self-reliant, rugged, and decisive.

I think that struggle continues on so long as there is the myth of opportunity. And I do think that has been historical reality in Texas and still is. For the people who come across the Rio Grande from Mexico, they see Texas as a land of opportunity still. But the opportunity is never quite as great as one's vision of

> **I think there are myths about Texas—that we're rugged, self reliant and decisive.**

the way things ought to be—or someone's vision of what could be. But I think one is looking for a new life. The reality is something else. So there's always a struggle going on, partly because of the myth of it being a land of opportunity. The struggle is always going on between the way things really are and the way things ought to be—or someone's vision of what could be. But I think it's that a very tension, which is so often determined on the side of opportunity. Opportunity may not have been as great as it once was or is perceived to be, but it was significant enough that people could invest themselves in it. And because folks wherever they are, whether they're entrepreneurs coming into Texas in 1830 or they are Hispanics coming across the river in 2005, have enough opportunity here that they do continue to come in. They see themselves as being rugged, self reliant and decisive, and find those qualities to have a positive effect for them. Now that struggle has played itself out in many different places and ways. I have experienced that between farmers and ranchers.

A story I like to tell is about the ranching folk I knew who at one time lived in Marfa, I met them in Del Rio. They'll like to tell about how in Marfa they would work hard all week long so on Saturday they could go dance. They would dance in El Paso, which was like four and a half hours away by pickup truck. As good church going folks they would dance into the wee hours of the morning and they'd drive that four and a half hours back from El Paso and be back for church bright and early for the first service in Marfa. But that just shows the adventuresome spirit and willingness to go the distance.

＊＊＊

When people who don't have this same sort of state identity say, "so you're from Texas, what's the big deal about that?", you have to come up with some response. By the way, I lived in Virginia and it is close to Texas in having a sense of self-identity. It's mostly whether or not you can trace your lineage back to someone who was in the Revolutionary War in the late 1700s—or possibly through the Civil War. But there were many people who were proud to be Virginians. But in Texas, yes, I have an identity as a Texan that I am pleased with. There are times when I'm embarrassed by that, where I see some Texan make a fool of himself and people say, "Aren't you a Texan too?" Like Saint Peter, I wanted to say, "never knew that feller."

My wife and I have had taco parties or Mexican food parties. We've invited other Texans to come and we eat Tex-Mex food together and we celebrate being Texans with one another. I'll tell you we've done that with people of all political stripes, all life style interests, but the thing that we all held in common was that we were all from Texas.

There was a sense of pleasure about recognizing that. We all have an identity. That identity is instilled in Texans. Each person's view of that identity may be slightly different, but there is an identity as a Texan. One carries that with them to another locale and celebrates it in the ways that we think are true to Texans—which in my experience has been found around food. Sometimes it's around dress. There are some individuals who would want, in these Texas gatherings, to wear their boots and hats. I never wore boots and hats and still don't to this day. I never accepted that part of the identity of Texas, the dress part, but I did accept the food part. So that's what I've used to celebrate my identity of other locales.

Although there is a Texas identity, I think there's even a regional Texas identity and I'm not certain that every Texan is aware of it as much as they are aware of the Texas identity. We are often identified as Texans wherever we go—we are not often identified as South Texans, East Texans or West Texans. For a person who has been in the state a while and met Texans from other parts of the state, we began to realize there are differences. My experience of that rugged individualistic, decisive nature that I think is a part of the Texas identity, is much more heightened in West Texas than it is in East Texas. East Texas, having much of its historical and cultural influence from the Old South, gives value to that group. I think in West Texas, the rugged individualistic strain is still quite strong and highly valued.

I remember an African-American fellow in Merkel who worked at a local plant. He was a butcher and meat cutter. At some point, he decided he wanted to be the sheriff. So he moved to a neighboring county, got appointed as a deputy sheriff and eventually ran for sheriff and was elected in a mostly white county. I figure the people did that because race was not such an issue as it was hard work. Was this fellow willing to work hard and keep his nose clean and respect other people in the community? That all goes with part of that Texas mentality, but because it is so much more prominent in West Texas, they were able to be freer to elect somebody different from their culture whose values really were the same as theirs.

Texas has several states within the state. Texas is large enough and culturally diverse enough so that is possible.

If Texas were to secede from The Union,
it would have the 8th largest economy in the world.

★ BIRTHPLACE ★
Sinton, TX

★ CURRENT RESIDENCE ★
Victoria, TX

★ OCCUPATION ★
Restaurant Owner

Peggy relates to the Mexican influence which is found throughout Texas.
The two cultures have always been closely tied together and that will remain.
The Mexican culture has influenced many of the customs and
traditions of Texas. Mexican food, for example, is as readily accepted by most
Texans as barbecue. The first official rodeo ever held was performed in Pecos, Texas.
The rodeo was born out of cattle handling skills originally displayed
by the Mexican vaqueros—the original cowboys. Texas has always been
and continues to be a melting pot of cultures.

The first thing that comes to me when you talk about Texas is freedom. Of course, we have laws and regulations, but as far as opinions and in speaking, we have that opportunity to speak our minds.

I like the weather of South Texas. I guess the beauty of Texas is that you have the wild flowers, the beautiful oak trees, pecan trees—just nature itself here in Texas is beautiful.

I love to go to beaches—water sites like Corpus (Christi). I like to go to San

Antonio—especially San Antonio—I feel more of the Mexican heritage there. It's a good place to learn more about your heritage. San Antonio is a place where I feel that more Hispanics have an opportunity to grow and make something of themselves.

The Hispanic community is very family oriented as a whole. I like being a Texan. But at times, depending upon what areas of Texas you're in, you get put down or get looked at differently. In fact, there is still discrimination against Mexican people in places.

The Lone Star Flag: the blue stands for loyalty,
the white represents strength, and the red is for bravery.

CAPT. CLARENCE LINCOLN CLARK

★ BIRTHPLACE ★
Anchorage, AK

★ CURRENT RESIDENCE ★
Corpus Christi, TX

★ OCCUPATION ★
Fishing Boat Owner & Captain

My first encounter with Captain Clark was when I was doing a Countryline Magazine *story about Drum fishing in the Gulf of Mexico. He operates a couple of boats off the T-heads in downtown Corpus Christi. He's a good example of Texans who came from somewhere else but have carved out a life for themselves and assimilated into the tapestry of Texas. By the way, if you have never caught a Drum, it's a real kick. Go try it. If I'm not right, call me. It's like trying to drag a Volkswagen off the bottom of the ocean. They run in Corpus Christi Bay from late February into April. It will wear you out.*

The diversity is what makes Texas special. It doesn't matter where you go in Texas, you'll find diversity. You go to West Texas—it's so different from East Texas. When you go up closer to Oklahoma, it's way different than South Texas. It's the diversity. That's what makes it unique to me. I'm lucky because I get to see all of it.

My wife is a mixture of Irish and Bo Hunk. So it doesn't get more hard headed than that. I think if you look throughout the state there's a whole lot

Thank goodness Uncle Sam brought us to Texas.

of that. Her grandparents came from Czechoslovakia. On her father's side, his daddy came over here from Ireland. You get them two people together that's some hard headedness right there. I think that has a lot to do with Texas. I think you find that a lot. It's the different mix of people. It may lead to a stubbornness—but these people are solid.

That ruggedness comes from a long way back. I don't think it ever left. I think Texans know that on any given day we could still secede the Union and probably do better than the rest of the country. We have more natural resources and more natural get up and go than most folks in other states can imagine. We send all of our natural gas north to keep the rest of the country warm. As far as agriculture goes, we've got it over everybody. As far as the oil industry goes, again, we've got it over everybody. And I think most Texans know it. I don't know if you call it a stuckupedness about it—knowin' it—or just a sense of pride. It's just like they said, "I might not have been born here, but I got here as quick as I could." My parents were both born in Massachusetts. That's the way they always felt about it. Thank goodness Uncle Sam brought us to Texas.

I'm a kind of an old beer hall, wooden floor kind of guy. I'm a little like that old Florie store up there by San Antonio. It says as much about Texas as anything. If you get there on the right night and there's a lot of dancing goin' on and the music is like it should be—a calm night—it's beautiful. I think everybody will tell you, they remember their family gathering at functions like that some time or other growing up. I think that's a big part of Texas. It's one of those things you hate to see go by the way. All of a sudden everything has gone so fancy—steel building nightclubs and all, you know. I think of places like Gruene Hall and Florie's store. That's a lot of what Texas is about.

With all of the movement now in Texas with the Texas music, musicians realize they don't have to go anywhere else. They can capitalize right here in Texas—Texas is plenty—and if they sell something somewhere else that's great, but Texas is plenty. Maybe some of that comes from that type of thinkin'. But I know a lot of them weren't born in Texas either. But they realized, "You know what? This is where it's at. This is where I want to make my music, this is the kind of music I want to make and this is the kind of place I want to live." Whatever happens anywhere else, they're not concerned. So that says a lot. It says a lot about the state and it says a lot about the people who come here and have lived here. I think most folks will tell you that they haven't seen enough of Texas. Me and my wife discuss it all the time. We talk about going and seeing more of Texas before we go see anything else.

It's amazing. It's just amazing when you get up around Dallas and see the growth north of Dallas goin' up toward Allen, Frisco, and Wylie—you see all those little towns going through these explosions.

You see Corpus Christi where we are right now, we're sitting on the verge of an explosion the way Houston did back in the late 1960s, early 1970s. We're sittin' in that place right now. Around three hundred thousand people in the surrounding area and know that when

this thing goes, it will probably go right quick to a million. From Corpus Christi south, we are The Valley. As much as people don't want to admit that, Corpus Christi's still part of The Valley, it is. It is the beginning of the end of the world.

It's funny, I get a kick out of talking to people from all over the country. "This is paradise," they say. And still there's nothing here. What you have to realize, we're the end of the world. Anything that's gonna happen here is going to be unique in itself and it'll make it because of that. It comes back around to being about individuals—being like the big cities is not in our mindset—we are who we are.

Amarillo is closer to four other states' capitols
than it is to its own.

BUDDY SCHLEY

★ BIRTHPLACE ★
Dallas, TX

★ CURRENT RESIDENCE ★
Canyon, TX

★ OCCUPATION ★
Retired lawyer, Clergyman and Judge

~ 🖊 ~

Here you get a sense of where Texans draw part of their identity.
It's not only the family values instilled at a young age, but how their surroundings
fill them with a sense of belonging to something bigger than themselves.

Tweed: In your opinion, what makes Texas special?

Buddy: I have lived in Florida, Tennessee, Virginia, and California and I think the people here are friendlier and more helpful to their neighbors than anyplace I have ever lived. That is not to say that they are bad people back there. There are very good people in those other places. Texas is just better. I have turned down promotions just to move back here.

Tweed: Is there something that comes to mind that ties Texas together?

Buddy: I think most of us take pride in the rich history of the state and the colorful characters who made that history, most of who had been run out, with good reason, of other states. It is a state of eccentrics.

Texas was a land of second chances originally. There were people who really did have problems where they were and came here for that reason. The problem may have been considered scandalous at the time—a divorce or maybe something a lot worse. Jim Bowie was accused of murder as I recall. One of my relatives that came here early on was accused of cattle rustling. I don't think he did, but who knows.

Tweed: What does it mean to you personally to be a native Texan?

Buddy: There is a sense of being part of something larger than yourself, a joy, and being able to laugh at yourself a lot.

Tweed: What about the majesty that is the Texas Panhandle?

Buddy: Well, in this part of Texas I love the sunrises and sunsets, the wide open spaces, the clear blue sky; that was true in Dallas when I grew up, but isn't true anymore. One of the things I heard the other day, I think on the radio, is that God saves his best artists to do the skies in Texas. That may be, I don't know.

There is just something about the landscape here. It is so flat and so long and yet the sky is so big. It is not just the space per se, but the diversity within that space, all the different cultures, all the different types of geography— the canyons, the rivers, the trees, the mountains, the coast. You can spend a lifetime and not exhaust the joy of this particular state.

Tweed: Is there anything else that you can think of that you want to pass along?

Buddy: Great people, that's the key. My grandfather was Roy Bryan. He was 6'4" at a time when most men were 5'8". His father was 6'7", one of the biggest men in the state of Texas. One of the things that my grandfather always emphasized was never measure a man by his height or his weight but by the size of his heart. He was a native Texan too. I thought that was pretty profound.

Texas has 254 counties, the most of any state in the country.

STEVE KERSH

★ BIRTHPLACE ★
Winnsboro, TX

★ CURRENT RESIDENCE ★
Amarillo, TX

★ OCCUPATION ★
Chief Meteorologist, KVII TV Channel 7, Amarillo, TX

Texas is a place that can experience virtually every weather phenomenon found anywhere on the planet. The weather and climate are often as diverse as the geography itself. The weather can turn from serene to majestically violent in minutes. The Panhandle of Texas is a wonderful place to watch the weather. A small morning cloud buildup on the horizon can mushroom into a ferocious thunderhead by afternoon. One storm can level large areas of towns or cities in their path. This meteorologist has spent many years observing this fearsome beauty.

I was born in a town called Winnsboro in northeast Texas. It's not where I lived though. My mom went to see my aunt while we were living in Sherman, Texas. Mom made a trip she wasn't supposed to in her ninth month of pregnancy and I was born in a town I never lived in. I lived in Sherman for eleven years and then moved to Clifton, Texas, just northwest of Waco. I'm a native Texan and have lived here all my life.

Coming from me, with a scientific point of view, we're one of the few states that have almost every single type of microclimate you can imagine. What I mean by that is in far East Texas—Texarkana, in the Piney Woods—the average rainfall is 60 inches a year. This is a dense forest type climate—a mold growth on everything. It's almost tropical. In El Paso they average around nine inches of rain a year, actually less than nine. This is considered a desert climate. So you can drive all day—and it will take you all day—and you can see both ends of the spectrum as far as climate goes.

We are also one of the few states to have big variances in elevation. You go from sea level around Houston, Galveston and Corpus Christi to nearly 9,000 ft at Guadalupe Peak. So we have a wide variation in elevation and climate, which lends to a uniqueness of weather. To get that 60 inches of rain you have to have water, rain and a lot of storms in East Texas. Then you have almost nothing in far West Texas. In between, you just run the gamut. You have sandstorms, blizzards in the Panhandle, tornadoes and then there are the hurricanes in the Gulf, dust storms in far West Texas. It's just unique in that you can see everything within one state's borders. In the rest of the U.S. if you want to see that type of tropical climate, you can go to Florida, Georgia, Mississippi, or Alabama. If you want desert climate, you have to go to Arizona or New Mexico. Here we have it all.

As far as people go, what I think that makes Texas unique is the pride the people have. We're one of the few places that by state law fly the Texas flag at the same height as the American flag. A lot of those things just kind of play into each other. Plus we're unique in that we have so much ethnic diversity in Texas. I came from a town in Clifton that is Norwegian. When I moved there I had no idea that people from Norway ever made it to Texas, but they did. We used to play a team in West, just north of Waco, that was all Czechoslovakian. In a way it was weird that in this little area you had a bunch of people from different countries. Yet, they're Texans.

My wife is from Albany, Texas, just northeast of Abilene. Fort Griffin was one of the Indian outposts there. There is a lot of history there too about how they would lose settlers daily to Comanche raids. There were a lot of things that were weather related against people too. That's why I think the Panhandle was one of the last places to be settled. A lot of the Indians were forced this way and the weather was absolutely unforgiving to folks. Some of the first settlers here lived in the ground. They lived in those little dugouts. That ought to tell you how bad it was. The wind was always blowin'; the snow was everywhere. It was a bomb shelter kind of existence. It was really rough. There were a lot of things playing against folks that wanted to settle here. That too may have instilled a lot of pride. "I moved here." "I lived here." "I survived it." That type of thing probably had something to do with that pride. There is independence in the mindset.

That's probably true of the Confederacy too—when they broke away from the

U.S., there was a sense of pride in that too—of independence. I took Texas history in college and one of the things that my professor at A&M said was that they probably would have broken away on their own even if the rest of the Confederacy hadn't asked them to join. It was just the fact they were so stubborn. There was a lot stubbornness in Texas—a lot of resistance to change in some cases.

There is one easy explanation of why you can see the whole storm up here in the Panhandle—lack of trees. Where I grew up we had some trees. There was a lot of cedar, a lot like Austin. We were on the northern edge of the Hill Country so there was a lot of cedar and some live oak. It's odd but once you get on top of the Caprock you lose the trees. And once you do that, all of a sudden you can see from horizon to horizon. We have some of the most beautiful sunsets and sunrises anywhere. A lot of it is due to lack of trees and lack of cover because as the sun is coming up lower on the horizon, much of the time you may not notice it when you have a bunch of trees and buildings around. But all of a sudden you're here and you can see. The running joke is, of course, that if you stand on one of the buildings in Amarillo you can see the back of your head looking the other way. I hear the same thing about Lubbock. It is flat. When I moved

> The running joke is, of course, that if you stand on one of the buildings in Amarillo you can see the back of your head looking the other way.

up here I always had a presumption that the Panhandle was flat from one side to the other. That's really not true. If you get up north of here in the Canadian River Valley, it is very pretty. Off the Caprock is amazing, especially around Canadian. It's like a lush little river valley there. It's called the Oasis of the Panhandle. There is a lot of topography that a lot of people don't know about. Yes, it is flat in spots. I mean deathly flat, but there are also some places like Palo Duro Canyon — you're just driving and all of a sudden the earth falls off.

Being a native Texan is one of those pride things. It's kind of funny to me too because when you speak of fifth generation Texans, there are a lot of Texans that will trace their families all the way back to the first Spanish explorers. We're only second generations Texans. My grandparents emigrated here from Mississippi. Even going further back than that the Kersh clan immigrated to South Carolina from Germany and made their way to Mississippi. Then apparently one side of the family was asked to watch a little girl who was playing on a swing. The girl fell out, hit her head and died. The family split in two. One went to Southeast Texas and my family is part of that group. The other went to Northwest Arkansas. I think David Kersh, the country singer is part of that second split, so we're

Of course, weather wise, my folks still think we live somewhere near the North Pole 'cause we live in the Panhandle.

indirectly related. My grandparents were not natives—both sides were not natives. It's just one of those things like I said that instills a pride to say, "Yes, I am a native Texan," I will say this though, it's seems to mean more to say that down state than it does in the Panhandle. That's the one thing I have noticed living in both places. I think it may have something to do with the fact that we're so close to New Mexico, Oklahoma, and Colorado.

Texans love their barbecue. It is a big deal. The barbecue down state is totally different from the barbecue in the Panhandle. My wife and I are big barbecue fans. We eat a lot of brisket, lots of sausage and chicken. We're fans. Down in Central Texas the sauce is a little more vinegary. Up here it's much more sweet and here they serve stewed apricots with barbecue plates. When my wife and I went to this barbecue place and they gave us apricots we thought, "What in the heck is that?" They also serve a different kind of meat. They serve shoulder clods. It's shoulder meat where down there it's strictly brisket. We've noticed this big change even from one side of the state to the other. I think a lot of it has to do with our location to Colorado, New Mexico—even the dialect is a little different up here than it is down state. There's much less

of a twang in the Texan dialect here than there is other parts of the state.

There is a tremendous difference from one side of the state to the other. Of course, weather wise, my folks still think we live somewhere near the North Pole 'cause we live in The Panhandle. When we go back home and I talk to folks, they say, "Oh, you work in Amarillo. Isn't it cold up there?" Well, not all the time. Hey, we're not Canada.

Even our temperature records are very extreme. Very few states have had the highest temperature ever recorded in Texas (123 degrees in Seymour, TX) and the record low is in Tulia with a minus 30 degrees. Very few states can have extremes like that so close to each other (about 200 miles a part). Texas is a tough place to forecast weather.

Frankly, the weather and tornadoes is what drew me here. When I grew up down in Waco, I studied weather since I was very little. My mom has a tape of when I was three of me tappin' on the wall of the kitchen with a yardstick talking about tornadoes and thunderstorms coming down from Oklahoma to Texas. I watched the TV weather every night. So they figured out real fast that was the way to punish me when I was beatin' up on my bothers. They wouldn't let me watch the six and ten o'clock weather.

The Panhandle has had the big tornadoes and they have the blizzards and they have the snow and they have the big hail. So for a meteorologist, working in Lubbock or Amarillo is really a coveted job. There is very little turn over as far as weather jobs because people nationwide have realized this. The TV stations here dedicate a lot of time and money—a tremendous amount of money—we have over a million and half dollars in weather equipment in our office. We wouldn't have had that if the weather were not as volatile as it is.

There have been occasions in which we've had tornadoes in the early afternoon—severe thunderstorms and tornadoes—and that night we have had snow. There are many, many documented cases of that happening. In some cases, a town that was hit by a tornado at two or three o'clock in the afternoon got six inches of snow that night. That's the kind of things that happen, but you end up asking yourself, "Where else are you going to see something like that?" There are very few places in the country where that can happen. Weather-wise it's a challenge, keeps us on our toes and makes life interesting for us. People here know too that we're never going to get it right all the time. They'll give their meteorologists that much leeway. But when things really start happening and we have a lot of storms going on and tornadoes on the ground, it's really interesting to be here because it is a life and death situation. We had one in Happy, Texas a couple of years ago. A couple didn't get out of their mobile home when they should. I was helping the weekend meteorologist who was doing the on air coverage that day. It hit him squarely between the eyes. He had to stop 'cause he kind of got choked up when he realized some people died on his watch. That's how seriously we take it. We consider ourselves like weather policemen—trying to protect the public as much as we can.

Something that a lot of folks may not realize about out area is that originally, the Panhandle of Texas went all the way up into Wyoming. It went through Colorado and New Mexico. So it's kind of strange to know that this area encompassed all that. I think because of all that some of the folks who have lived here the longest still retain some of that heritage. Folks here seem to be a little more blended with their surroundings. Even our fair is a Tri State fair. They try to encompass the surroundings too. Even the panhandle of Oklahoma feels a lot less attached to the rest of Oklahoma than they do Texas. If Texas would ask them, "Would you like to join the party?" I bet they'd go for it.

I went to Guymon, Oklahoma one time and heard there are still some folks up there who are kind of upset that the folks in the Texas Panhandle call themselves the Panhandle. Technically we're not the "pan handle," they are. The one thing the Oklahomans tend to resent is the fact that we call ourselves the Panhandle. It may not be the majority, but the opinions have been expressed.

Something you may not have known, the New Mexico legislature has filed a bill that they are going to pursue here next year. They intend to fight Texas. It is their contention that the parallel that runs from Dalhart all the way down to near Wink was actually drawn the wrong way. What this will do if they draw it to that parallel is that it's going to put four Texas towns in New Mexico. Texline is one of them. Farwell is another. These are all going to become New Mexico. People are not happy about it. It's a big deal and has sparked a bunch of who-are-you-loyal-to. Plus, there's no state tax in Texas and there is in New Mexico. New Mexico stands to gain thousands of square miles but a lot of it will just be rangeland. There are a couple of towns involved. It's argued by New Mexico that the parallel is somewhat diagonal right now, not straight. They want to straighten out that parallel, which of course, the farther out you go the more land you get. That's why all of a sudden, the whole town of Texline would be in it, but down by Wink there wouldn't be much at all. They say the surveyor who drew that line, drew it incorrectly. Because of that they claim that they lost land and Texas gained land and they want it back. If it does happen, it will affect a lot of things, even the time zones.

BIFF BOBNEY

★ BIRTHPLACE ★
Houston, TX

★ CURRENT RESIDENCE ★
Nacogdoches, TX

★ OCCUPATION ★
Art Teacher

This interview came out of that late afternoon thunderstorm sitting on the veranda of a big two-story farmhouse out in the country near Nacogdoches. I was speaking with Bill Roberts, Jerry Jernigan, Reagan Patton and this man, Biff Bobney. I consider this conversation a gem. You get a sense of how comfortable one can be being a Texan.

Texas is such a multi-faceted state that I really don't know where to start to describe it. I like to let my art speak for the way I feel about Texas. I did a Texas collage that has the background of the Texas flag, the Alamo and Spindletop, the first oil well in Texas. It has some of our humor—the giant jackrabbit with a cowboy riding it. When we were kids and we went into tourist places, we'd see the postcards like that.

Texans are many things. They're cocky. They're Hell with the hide tore off. You sure want them to be on your side. It's kind of like the Texas Rangers' motto: a man in the wrong can't stand up to a man in the right who just keeps on a-comin'. And that's what Texans do.

A Texan has a sense of humor.
A Texan is not afraid to cry.
A Texan is not afraid to die.
Can you tell I'm very proud to be a Texan?

Texas is an attitude. I think you're born with the Texas attitude. It's that gene you're talking about. See, I'll be the fifth generation to have this property. It's like *Gone With The Wind*, the red dirt of Tara that was so important to Scarlet.

We're sitting here on a hill and you can imagine how this looked two or three hundred years ago. In those days it was Caddo Indians that lived here. So, the whole point I'm trying to make is that being a Texan, it's a way of life. For example, there's nothin' more humorous than seeing a movie or TV show or a celebrity trying to act like a Texan. You know the ones I'm talking about. He comes to Texas and they take him to a western wear shop. He has no idea how to properly dress like a Texan or how to style a hat properly.

A Texan has a sense of humor. A Texan is not afraid to cry. A Texan is not afraid to die. Can you tell I'm very proud to be a Texan?

Knowing that I'm a Native Texan means that I was blessed, that God blessed me and that I'm able to live here in Nacogdoches, the oldest town in Texas. I'm an hour away from Longview, two hours away from Houston, three hours

from Dallas. I can get on a plane and leave, but I always want to come back to Texas. It's like sleepin' in your own bed.

Texans are very humble people. They learned how to restore lost honor. And they're very boisterous, arrogant and they often let their alligator mouth overload their canary ass. But they're great people. They are some of the funniest too. A Texan is the type of person who will stop and help somebody on the side of the road and they won't expect anything in return. They'll go out of their way for people. Texans will welcome you into their home with hospitality. People won't let you go hungry. You know, my casa is your casa. They just make you feel welcome.

Texas is kind of like a crazy quilt. It's a hodge-podge. A potpourri of wit, humor, tradition and sincerity. It's a way of life. We're not just playin' Texan. We are Texan. We're a very proud people. Sometimes being a Texan will get you in trouble. A lot of people are jealous of Texans. Lots of people wish they were from Texas.

When Davy Crockett wrote home to his wife, he wrote that this was the "emerald place of the world." It was probably when it was cool and not humid in East

Texas. Can you imagine what those people went through, how it must have looked with Indian trails like El Camino Real and how people got from place to place? Imagine how tough they had to be and the fortitude and the tenacity they had to have.

A true Texan is like someone out of *Lonesome Dove*. I called my friend Reagan and told him my dad died and the first thing he did—he come a runnin'. That's what friends do. They help and support each other when a lot of people give up on you. They see the good in you.

I can come out here and feel good karma and good vibes. I think that's how Texas is. It's like that old pair of house shoes you got or that La-Z-Boy recliner or that mattress. It just fits.

Today approximately 22 million people live in Texas, only slightly outnumbering its 15 million cattle. Texas is also home for about 2.5 million deer and 200,000 alligators.

TIMELESS TRADITIONS and CUSTOMS

EMILIANO QUINTERO

★ BIRTHPLACE ★
El Campo, TX

★ CURRENT RESIDENCE ★
Victoria, TX

★ OCCUPATION ★
Truck Driver

I met Emiliano during a trip to Victoria, Texas. I was taken by his upbeat view.
He recognized the abundance of the natural resources, but notice how quickly
he turned to another natural resource in Texas: her people.

hat puts Texas on the map are the resources we have — including the history. The first thing people think of when they hear Texas is oil. Oil, cattle, opportunity and whatever goes with it. Plus also the heritage that goes with it 'cuz there's a lot of history in Texas.

In my opinion, there are two nationalities when it comes to Texan and Mexican cultures. I think because there's Mexican Texans, so to speak, and the other forms of Texans. So there is a difference. Many consider us Mexican Americans and there are other words that people use to describe us. But we're all Mexican Americans.

The Mexican heritage—where we went in Mexico—was much different. How people live there, as compared to how we live here, makes you think about how precious life is on this side. It makes you grateful for what you have over here. Again, it's the difference in opportunity.

It brings my spirits up when people ask me "Where you from?" I say I'm from Texas and I love it. It's the best state in The Union. I love being from Texas. It is where I was born and raised and when God takes me away, Texas is where I'm going to die.

When they talk about the history of Texas, it makes me feel more proud that I am a Texan. In some schools they may teach you about Pennsylvania or some other state and that's fine, but when they talk about Texas, people realize that Texas is good. They can think about moving down here. The history of Texas is wonderful.

What I love about this area is the people who live in this part of Texas. They're all friendly. They'll practically take the shirt off their back for you. The opportunities are out there for work in whatever line you want to get in.

Texas is one of the biggest states in The Union and I would advise anybody if they want to move somewhere, Texas is the place.

The highest paved road in Texas is on Mount Locke
in the Davis Mountains of West Texas.
It is 6,791 feet above sea level.
At the end of the road is the McDonald Observatory.

SUSIE KELLY FLATAU

★ BIRTHPLACE ★
Fort Sill, Oklahoma

★ CURRENT RESIDENCE ★
Austin, Texas

★ OCCUPATION ★
Author, www.WordsBySusie.com

Susie is a fellow author of Texana. She has written some wonderful
books about Texas. One is called Red Boots & Attitudes, *a collection of interviews*
with several Texas women. She also wrote Reaching Out to Today's Kids *and*
Counter Culture Texas, *where she traveled all over Texas and stopped at various*
lunch counters and talked to the locals. Susie is working on two new books—
Quotable Texas Women *and* Historic Texas Depots. *Flatau travels extensively*
as a speaker and workshop facilitator. I knew she would understand
what I was trying to accomplish.

O n one level, I see the Texas spirit as this beautiful compilation of stories from each Texas woman and man. And when I think of all of those stories, I know the Texas spirit is tied directly to the people. Clarissa Pinkola Estés, in her book The *Creative Fire*, talks about *el duende*, which is the spark or creative fire that fuels the human spirit. Ms. Estés also talks about how out of *el duende* comes a person's story. For me, the combined spirits of each and every Texan figuratively create one gigantic spark—one Texas-size *el duende*—and from that come the legends that are larger than life.

The second image that pops into my head is this network of roads that crisscross the state. There seems to be a rhythm that is created by this conglomeration of country roads, farm-to-market roads, highways and Interstates. It's invigorating to think you can travel hundreds of miles throughout Texas without ever crossing the state line. You can start in El Paso and head east to Center, or drive west from Newton to Sierra Blanca. You can drive north from Brownsville to Gainesville, or south from Perryton to Del Rio. Regardless of the direction you choose, the roads carry you to every nook and cranny in the state. I love that you can "go the distance" without ever leaving your home territory. Truly, the seemingly endless roads feed the human spirit.

> It's easy to meet Texans— to sit with them and swap life stories.

You know, I often hear newcomers talk about how they're embraced by every Texan they meet. They talk about how quickly they're welcomed into various circles. I have to agree. It's easy to meet Texans—to sit with them and swap life stories. By their very nature, I'd say that Texans are hospitable people. I think their generous hospitality comes from being comfortable in their skin and

from having this deep sense of belonging to a place.

It doesn't matter if you're talking about "city folk" or "country folk," everywhere you go in the state you find similarities in the Texas persona, the Texas spirit. Really. There is this ubiquitous "every-Texan" that can be found.

Let me tell you a story that captures the generosity of what I call the "every-Texan." My husband, Jack, is from Tonawanda, New York, a small town outside of Buffalo. He's often asked how he ended up living in Texas, and I never get tired of listening to his story.

After Jack graduated from a New York university, his oldest brother, Larry, and his sister-in-law, Kathy—who lived in Houston at the time—invited him to visit. Shortly after the invitation, Jack won a football pool sponsored by a local newspaper. So with this extra cash, he decided to head for Texas. Just for the heck of it, he also applied for teaching jobs in and around Houston.

As fate would have it, within a month Jack received a phone call from an elementary principal in Kingwood (Texas) who offered him a teaching position. Ever the spontaneous sort, Jack accepted right then and there. When he hung up the phone, he realized he was moving to Texas! "Texas!" But in his mind he saw the move as temporary. That makes me smile. You see, he came to

Texas in the summer of 1979, and he's still here!

But let me get back to the story. Not long after Jack accepted the job, he loaded up his baby blue convertible Galaxy 500, kissed his mama goodbye, and began his journey. After driving for sixteen hours, he decided to grab some shut-eye at a rest stop located some seventy miles outside of Little Rock, Arkansas. Now you have to realize that he had never experienced southern heat, or humidity, or bugs. Needless to say, Jack quickly decided to get back on the road. He turned the key in the ignition—nothing. There he was—a long way from home—with his broken-down, baby blue convertible with New York license plates at a rest stop in Arkansas at nine o'clock on a muggy August morning. Things weren't looking so good.

But before long, a station wagon pulled up alongside Jack's car. Inside sat a young couple and their newborn baby—all headed to Dallas (Texas). Here's where Jack encountered his first experience with Texas generosity. The driver didn't think twice about stopping to offer his help. Within minutes, he and Jack were tinkering with the convertible engine—but no luck. Then this Texan—unfortunately, Jack cannot recall his name—drove his family and Jack the seventy miles to Little Rock where they bought a tow hitch. They returned to the rest stop, hitched up the convertible, and headed for Dallas. Now you have to remember, this man and his family did not know Jack from Adam, and it was a good four to five hundred miles to their Texas home.

When they finally reached Dallas, it was nightfall. Jack was invited to eat dinner and spend the night, and he accepted—"these strangers," he says, "already felt like family." The next morning, even before Jack was out of bed, his host had taken the day off from work and called around to locate parts for the convertible. By noon they had that convertible up and running. Jack's offer to help pay for car parts was refused. Instead, all that was asked of Jack was that one day he return the favor to someone in need.

I think about that story—how it captures Texas generosity. You know, it's truly overwhelming how the people of this bigger-than-life state have hearts that are bigger-than-life.

I guess because of this "bigger-than-life" quality, you can say that "Texas" is really a code word for "attitude." I believe that when you are born into or grow up in territory as big as Texas, your heart simply expands in proportion to the size of the land. Your arms are able to open wider and wider. You know, Texans are so connected to the land and its history that their pride runs deep—like a taproot. Wide and deep. That's what I think of when I think of the Texas attitude—wide arms and deep roots.

⊷⊶

While working on *Counter Culture Texas* back in 1996 with Mark Dean, a friend and photographer out of Houston, we spent time traveling Texas section-by-section. Of course, I had previously vis-

Where else but in Texas can you find so many nuggets of human gold in one giant-sized mother lode?

ited West Texas and the Panhandle, but I had never spent much time out west. Basically, I had never absorbed the true flavor of its land and people. Guess you could say I had always "passed through" on the way to Colorado or New Mexico. Anyway, while working on that book, the slow pace of West Texas came to the forefront of our observations. It didn't matter if it was a small or large town—there was a gentle current to life. Maybe it was the long lazy drives to the nearest diner or gas station? Or the straight, solitary roads stretching as far as the eye could focus? Whatever the case, life chugged along like a slow-moving train. I came to understand that the red-orange canyons, and the purple-blue hills, and the rare rain showers are precious to West Texans. That the rugged land is truly precious to them. But come to think on it, I believe you can say that all Texans treasure their land.

Of course, West Texas makes up only one part of the Lone Star profile. Down south, in the Rio Grande Valley, there is this delicate marriage of old and new worlds. As you drive through the area, you can observe thick, tall rows of sugar cane and low, sweeping fields of aloe vera plants that are flourishing alongside contemporary industrial growth. You find local mom-and-pop business-

es co-existing with "big box" establishments. Then there is the central slice of the "Texas pie." In this region, life picks up speed. A pulsating energy drives modern development and commercial ventures. Steel and glass structures rise like monoliths into the Texas sky. Yet despite it all, you are never far from the sanctuary of rolling violet hills and abundant rivers and lakes.

And last, but far from least, there is East Texas. Since I spent a great deal of my childhood visiting my mama's relatives in this part of the state, the Piney Woods have a special spot in my heart. For me, East Texas is a mysterious and mythical place. It is a place that offers the fascination of towering trees, boggy creeks, Caddo Lake, and Indian lore. Nature feels primitive and pristine. The forest floor gives like thick carpet beneath your feet. The dense air is filled with the smell of sweet earth. The rust-tinted, iron ore dirt colors the landscape. And amid all of this beauty, East Texans go about their daily lives to the speed of the unfolding seasons, to the rhythm of the evolving natural world.

All in all, it is exciting that a person—whether they are a native or a visitor—can experience the vast differences offered by the various regions within the Texas borders. And it is equally as thrilling that each of those unique and individual regions generates its own stories, its own characters. Where else but in Texas can you find so many nuggets of human gold in one giant-sized mother lode?

League City's population hovered around 5,000 people—give or take a hundred or so folks. I guess you could say it was typical of "small-town Texas." League City was a magical playground. My friends and I could ride bicycles around the entire town. We could trick-or-treat up and down every street at Halloween. We could walk to the picture show and soda fountains without the threat of being kidnapped or harmed. Another special aspect of my growing-up years was that I had the good fortune of knowing both farmers and astronauts. So I think about that, how growing up in League City provided me with opportunities not only to play in parsley fields but also to work as a tele-type operator for NASA during the 1969 Apollo mission. My childhood memories are good ones, strong ones.

The rural population of Texas is greater than the combined populations of Alaska, Delaware, North Dakota, Vermont and Wyoming.

HOWARD BOYD

★ BIRTHPLACE ★
Breckenridge, TX in Stephens County

★ CURRENT RESIDENCE ★
Amarillo, TX

★ OCCUPATION ★
Retired Meat Packer

One of the two basic questions I asked was, "What does it mean to you personally
to be a native Texan?" I was amazed how many times I would get the
"deer in the headlights look." Unbelievably, about half of the natives, when asked
that question, did not have a clue how to answer it. They really didn't know
because they have lived their whole life here and didn't have any other
frame of reference to compare it to.

I really wouldn't know why Texas is different. I never lived anywhere else. But I'm satisfied with this. It means quite a bit to me to live in Texas. I'd rather live in Texas than any other place. I like the people, how the state government runs the state. I like the weather, mostly—the sunrises and sunsets.

JOHN "J.C." ESLINGER

★ BIRTHPLACE ★
Denver, Colorado

★ CURRENT RESIDENCE ★
Dallas, TX

★ OCCUPATION ★
Aviation Consultant

If there is a more interesting man in Texas, I haven't met him yet. J. C. Eslinger in a sense,
found me. My publisher, Sylvia, had attended a wedding of a relative in Atlanta. There she
noticed a short man with a distinguished handlebar mustache wearing a cowboy hat.
Sylvia is not shy. She walked up to him and asked if he was from Texas. "Yes ma'am, I am,"
he said with a beaming grin. An instant friendship had begun. She called me and told me
that I needed to talk to this guy. I agreed but before I could call him, he called me.
He was glad to be a part of this project. A short time later he drove to Austin from Dallas
for our interview. Another friendship was born. You cannot help but like this man—
his spirit and sense of Texas is irrepressible.

I moved within a few months of my birth to Texhoma, right on the Texas-Oklahoma border. We lived on the Texas side. My mother owned the laundry on the Oklahoma side. So I got to experience some of the ambiance of the Okies by default. There is a psychological border with Oklahoma. I've seen it many times.

I think two things make Texas different and unique. First, it's a mental insight—a logical thing. The other thing is that it's a physical thing, which is based on the size of Texas and the type of geography, the character of the people that settled this place and made it what it is. There's another thing, too, that is more prolific in the world, the image of Texas portrayed in television and movies. The TV show Dallas is still in syndication all over the world. It's amazing, in almost every country I've been to—and I have been to over 40 countries—everybody knows about Texas. And in a lot of ways, it's kind of a warped look at us. People ask me, "Do you I own a horse?"

I tell them, "No".

Then they ask, "Can you ride a horse?"

"Absolutely."

"Do you own an oil well?"

"I wish," [he says with a chuckle].

"Do all Texans own oil wells?"

"No, only the oil companies."

Yeah, the image has really been created by the media and the movies in the last 30 or 40 years. Before that, it was more of a legend passed on by word of mouth and print.

I have been really blessed. I've been to every piece of Texas. The way I think about it is you have East Texas with the Piney Woods and you've got West Texas where they have twelve trees. I've really given this some serious thought.

When you live in East Texas you've got lots of trees—they're tall. When you live in Central Texas, you have the Hill Country and there's lots of trees but they're not as tall as the trees in East Texas. East Texas is really green. The Hill country is fairly green. West Texas ain't green. I really think there is something about colors that has something to do with the way people think. That might be a good study for somebody. I can't stand to be in East Texas too long because all you see is green. I feel constricted. Yet, people who live in East Texas feel exposed when they get out into West Texas. At least you can see who's gonna get you in West Texas.

If you go up into the Panhandle, it's one of the flattest places on earth and the wind blows all the time. Here again, the wind affects the way you think. I can prove it too, but I have to stand up to show you. This is almost a truism and a bit of an exaggeration. When I moved from Amarillo to Austin, I stood like this (leaning slightly forward) because if I didn't stand like this, the wind would blow me over. Seems like for the first six months, until I got acclimated, everybody thought I was handicapped. Another thing too, you know that Chicago is called the windy city, but I read in a magazine that listed the six windiest cities in the United States that first is Amarillo, Texas and the sixth one was Chicago. The wind blows in Amarillo on the average of fourteen miles an hour 24/7/365. After leaving there and moving to Austin, I thought I'd died and gone to geographical heaven.

The interesting thing about living in the Panhandle and watching the weather is you can watch those big majestic storms grow from scratch. Watch it from when it's just a tiny little cumulus until it's gone through it's complete cycle. I must admit, I miss that. Learning how to fly in Amarillo was great. The wind was always high and it was always sideways.

Another thing that separates the regions of Texas—not only the sight and scenery and the color green versus brown—is the major metropolitan areas. For instance, Dallas is truly a big, slick, shiny city. It really could be the Manhattan of Texas. The other problem with Dallas is there's just too damn many Yankees there. What I find really intriguing about Dallas is you hardly ever see anybody wearing a cowboy hat. If you wanna see cowboy hats you go to Fort Worth. I love Fort Worth—I'd be happy to live in Fort Worth because the people there are more laid back—laid back and wired at the same time. It has more pickup trucks and the people are friendly. I believe, and this is not to denigrate anyone else, Texas really starts on the east side city limits of Fort Worth. When you drive from Fort Worth going west, it is instantly what you think Texas is. It's rolling ground, mesquite bushes, and really rugged terrain. There are lots of farms, and cows, and horses and lots of oil between Fort Worth and Abilene too.

Everybody I know that knows anything about Texas history thinks the same thing.

For me the Alamo is kinda like the Vatican. The Alamo still affects me the same way it did the first time I walked into it. You don't have to have anyone tell you that you're some place special.

Every human wants to have something that makes them be a little special about whatever—whether it's your religion or position in the family. I've noticed that in almost every culture I've ever visited. When I look around at all the things that make our country special, I look at Texas and think, "Man this is it." You go to Massachusetts and a few people are waving the Massachusetts flag as if to say, "Hey I'm from here." I know I can be ragged on for my size, some people might say, "Well, I thought everything was big in Texas, what happened to you?" and I tell 'em, "It's not about big. It's a mental thing." I feel like it is my opportunity to be uniquely individualistic within a group. I think most Texans feel the same way. It's even true for imported Texans. I was talking to one lady on the phone making reservations yesterday in Houston. She grew up in Houston and lives in Tomball. She said, "I'm a Texan and that's all I ever wanna be."

I think I was blessed to grow up out west and get raised around horses and know how to ride. I grew this cool mus-

> For me
> the Alamo is
> kinda like
> the Vatican.

tache and that kind of makes me fit in. I've always worn hats and really feel like a real Texan. The only time I didn't was when I played the corporate game to get where I needed to be.

Texas is all about attitude. One thing made it simple for me to understand early on—I grew up in this town where half of it was in Oklahoma of the other half, in Texas. There was always this friendly competition between the Oklahoma side and the Texas side— plus we had to study Texas history. The Okies didn't study Texas history so they didn't have a clue. They were nice folks, but Oklahoma was still considered somewhat of a no-man's land. So I learned early on that I'm from Texas and that makes me special. That was the attitude on my side of town. The

thing that made it so important was that we learned about the Alamo when we were little bitty kids. We learned about Davy Crockett and Texas history. So just by osmosis, for lack of a better term, we got inculcated with all this stuff just by being there. I'd bet 90 per-cent of the people I grew up with on the Texas side feel just like me. They've diluted the situation now—it's one of the only places in the whole country where they have such cooperation between two states. When I was going to school there, the elementary school was on the Texas side. You went first through the sixth grade on the Texas side. Then you had to go to the Oklahoma side to go to junior high and high school. The states had some kind of reciprocal agreement. I left when I was just about to go to the Oklahoma

Well, if you come down and you want to mess with Texas, it won't be long before you're gonna wanna leave.

side. Boy that was close. It really was a big deal to us to live in Texas.

I was in China a few weeks ago and I saw this Chinese dude wearing a Dallas Cowboy sweatshirt. In China! It was obvious this guy was a native Chinese. I was really curious to know how he got his sweatshirt, but my Chinese is probably a lot like his English. So, I never asked him.

There are a couple of things that make Texans as friendly as they are. One, this is something we have inherited from the first generation of Texans. It was so tough to live. They had to stick together. Actually that's kind of the Western thing, Arizona's that way too, but they don't have the things that make Texas, Texas. People are just friendlier. The other thing is something that has almost turned into the state motto, "Don't mess with Texas". Well if you come down and you want to mess with Texas it won't be long before you're gonna wanna leave. In the meantime, everyone is going to treat you friendly and be nice to you. I think it's a way of making life easier and simple for everybody. You treat people the way you wanna be treated. I just think that's the Texas way. People really appreciate that and as a result you don't have as much conflict as you would if

you were being arrogant and like a Yankee. I have spent a lot of time in my life up in the Northeast.

Also I like to think I'm a goodwill ambassador to the world from Texas. So when I go to Yankee land—I'm there a lot—I am so friendly and so nice. I tip my hat to the ladies and you know what? They love it. I find all these people who were so hard nosed toward me and as soon as I say something, Texas comes rollin' out. It's real and they dig it. I treat them nice and friendly. It ain't long before I have a bunch of new friends. For the most part, Texans treat outsiders that way. The buttheads can just leave.

Let me run something by you. Australia is the only continent that I have not been to. However, I do have a lot of Australian friends. As a result, I have learned a lot about Australia. I think Texas is a lot like Australia. Australia was colonized by the British government by dumping prisoners, criminals, and renegades who were tough, hardy, and mean. It was a penal colony. They were full of the "can do" mindset. Look at Texas, and I rest my case. I traced my family history. My dad was born in Tennessee and when I look at the rest of the family, there were some characters. I really think my grandfather moved to no-man's land in 1906. He was running from somebody. Almost anybody you talk to who has traced their family roots back, if they came from the East, it seems most likely that they were running from somethin'. I really think somewhere all those genes got mixed together that somehow created a special gene—a T-gene. It has to be there.

— ◦—≡◦— —

I played the corporate game from January 1966 until 1993—dress code, white shirt, tie, the whole thing. It's funny, after I grew my mustache back, got out of the Italian loafers and into some cowboy boots, I felt like I got my identity back. You know, right away, my whole life changed. That's when I got the first hat I had owned in years. In fact, Suzanne, my wife, signed us up for the Hopalong Cassidy Festival. It's on his birthday, usually the first weekend in May in Cambridge, Ohio. We went to this festival and they had an auction. Suzanne found a hat and said I should bid on it. I got it for five bucks. I took it

to Peters Brothers in Fort Worth and had 'em reblock it. It is a cool lookin' hat. When I started wearing that hat, it totally changed my life. The last ten years has really been cool. You've got to be proud to your own pride.

I just came back from China and the form asks for your nationality. I put Texan and then I put USA in parentheses. It just cracks them up. When I walk in wearing cowboy boots and a hat, they know. I have never had anybody be put off by that.

When I travel around the world and meet people in foreign countries who have such an interest in Texas, I give them a certificate my wife made up with calligraphy making them honorary Texans. That really makes them smile.

I just know it's been one hell of a ride. When I get to the pearly gates, the way I got it figured is like this: Slide up to the front gate and jump out of my truck and say "Holy ^%&#. What a ride!" I just know "The Man" understands.

— ◦—≡◦— —

77 percent of Texas' counties (196) are classified as rural counties. 85 percent of the incorporated cities in Texas have a population of 10,000 or less.

JOHN KELSO

★ BIRTHPLACE ★
Maine

★ CURRENT RESIDENCE ★
Austin, TX

★ OCCUPATION ★
Humor Columnist for Austin American-Statesman
Newspaper & Author of the book, Texas Curiosities

John Kelso and I went to the same high school in Laconia, New Hampshire.
Most folks in Austin just assume he is a "Bubba from South Austin."
He is the longtime humor columnist for the Austin American-Statesman. *He is a hoot.*
I admire him too. The reason I wanted him for this volume was his keen sense
of observation. He drove all over the state looking for those weird side and back road
attractions that you will not find anywhere else on the planet but you will find
in his book Texas Curiosities. *I empathize with him. I drove all over this state too.*
It's fun but not for those who tire easily.

I think there's more state pride here than there is in any other state. There ain't too many other states where you can buy so much stuff shaped like the state. You know, there's key chains and everything else shaped like Texas. Most people, when they think of where they are from, don't think of it as being that big of a deal. When I was up in Maine a few years ago, I went looking for a University of Maine hat—they just won the NCAA championship. I was around Portland and a guy said, "You have to drive all the way to Orono." That would never happen in Texas. In Texas, if you ever wanted anything, you can find it all over the state. But a lot of states don't think of themselves in that way. I'd hate to do a book of *Delaware Curiosities*.

People here love to bulldoze and pave over. It's a more of a we-can-do-stuff-here attitude than there is in a lot of other places. Sometimes that's good and sometimes it's not. But, ah, they're the kind of people that rather than sit around and try to think of reasons not to do something—which I found was often the case in New England when I was growing up—they would rather think of reasons to do something. They'll go try something, like put in a business and see how it goes. Never tell a Texan he can't. He'll do it. Texans are the kind of people who don't mind changing a flat at one o'clock in the morning.

The state motto is: Friendship. It was adopted in 1930.
The word Texas is derived from the Indian word
"Tejas" meaning friend or ally. A coincidence?

ROGER MOORE

★ BIRTHPLACE ★
Beaumont, Texas

★ CURRENT RESIDENCE ★
Spicewood, Texas

★ OCCUPATION ★
Advertising Executive & Cartoonist
Creator of the Bonafide Original Texas Calendar

Texas Independence Day is a big deal in Texas. Each year an organization
called "Celebrate Texas" puts on a big parade in downtown Austin.
There are speeches, a chili cook-off, a golf tournament, children's essay
and picture contests and an abundance of parties both large and small—
all to celebrate a unique point in history. Roger is on the board of directors
for the group whose sole purpose is to encourage and promote the education
of the public regarding Texas Independence Day and the history of Texas.

He is also a talented cartoonist. Each year he sells Texas calendars chuck full
of his cartoons and the significant Texas dates. What makes these calendars so unique and
collector items is that the first day of the year is March second. Texas Independence Day.
It all begins in Texas on that day. Roger is a Texas gentleman by every definition of the term.
Every time he is introduced to a lady, he either tips or removes his cowboy hat
as he greets them. He's a class guy. He's Texan to the core.

The first time I was asked what made Texas special, it stumped me. I had to think about it for a while and I called my friend Mike Cox who is a Texas author and authority on the Texas Rangers. Here you have the feeling of independence and the pioneer spirit. The people who settled Texas were not wusses. They were tough stock and although we are several generations removed from that, we still have pioneer stock in us. We can, by God, do anything. People who were born and raised in Texas don't have a lot of limits. And what's unique about Texans is they don't care what you think. The people I know who are good solid Texans don't care what you think. They're not in it for your approval. They're doin' what they're doin' because they want to do it. If they make money at it, great. If they don't, they're still doin' what they want to do. Attitude is what separates us because we're not all that far removed from people who came here even in the twenties and thirties. Those were pioneers too—people who came to a rough ol' country. If you don't believe it, go out to Abilene and think about how it was to farm in the twenties and thirties out there. There were plenty of tough people less than a hundred years ago.

I asked my dad one time why he was a farmer and rancher. He said, "I don't like anybody tellin' me what to do. It's worth it to me not to answer to anybody. Even if I don't make as much money as someone sellin' shoes on the square in town or the pharmacist. I'd just rather have nobody tellin' me what to do."

Texas has always seemed to be tied to opportunities and struggles. They go hand in hand. You give up something every time you take chances. You leave something behind. You leave security behind and you take chances and there you've got the struggle. Again, that's the kind of people who settled this land. The people who are still doing well here and will be remembered here are the people who took it on the chin, got up and did it again. Look at the elements alone, lawlessness in the early days, Indians who didn't want us here in the first place—I don't blame 'em. It's a neat place to live. But it was tough. I'm seeing a return in the last four or five years of people examining why they're proud of Texas. I never was forced to answer that question until a couple of years ago. It disturbed me. I didn't know what made us different, but I think I've got a handle on it now.

Celebrate Texas is a unique organization started by Jay Johnson about five years ago. He called me one day and asked if I wanted to have a little fun. I said, "Sure." He had one of my calendars and said let's make Texas Independence Day an event again. I said, "Hey that's great—that's when my calendar starts."

He said, "Yeah, I know—that's the reason I asked you."

He wanted to get it where everyone remembered March 2nd with a parade and a Capitol celebration, make it like it used to be. People are tickled to death to be in Texas. Just celebrate one day a year and realize what a neat, neat place we have. Then maybe they'll start looking into the history of it and why it's a reason to be proud. We are the only state that was once a republic. If you go to Europe and draw a picture of the outline of the state of Kansas and an outline of the state of Texas—you'll see which one gets recognized. We are different and we are special. Texas Independence Day is a good time to focus on that and enjoy being a Texan, and being in Texas whether you're a Texan or not. If you live here, you're a Texan. We want more good people down here. It's funny how we say down here. That's an interesting way to talk about Texas.

Being a Native Texan? Well, you know, here's the honest to God's truth, it didn't mean a lot to me until I hit about forty. I never thought about it. I never thought much about where I came from or my history, being a part of this place that was forged out of nothin' and done so well. When you talk about Texas as a success story, you talk about people who came down here to get away from things, wanting a better life, takin' chances—they're still doing that. Texas still has that feel to it. One of the things that is so neat about it is that it's got a great history. Just think about what we're going to be in 50 years or 20 years for that matter.

> The spirit didn't catch up with me until I slowed long enough to pay attention.

Who'd a thought 30 or 40 years ago that a place like Austin would be the huge city it is today? Dallas, Houston—think of all we've gone through—innovating, invigorating—I'm just proud to be part of the success story. Texas is a success story—an ongoing success story at that. It was in the 1800s and even the late 1700s, and it has continually been a fine place to be. If you want to live in an invigorating place, you're here.

Like all kids, I knew about Davy Crockett and the Alamo. The Disney version struck me pretty hard. I knew somethin' stirred in me and I was always proud of the Texan imagery, but I didn't get comfortable with the Texas spirit until I was about forty. I didn't catch that spirit. I love the imagery. I loved the Alamo—always felt reverence whenever I went there. Catchin' the spirit came when I realized where I was and where I'd been and where I could go—a place like this—with all the history and the strength that's all around you, a real can do spirit. That's when it hit me. But I've always been in love with the mystique of it. The spirit didn't catch up with me until I slowed long enough to pay attention.

I will say that Texas can take in anybody. One of the sayings that we have for our Celebrate Texas crew is: Together We Are Texas. Anybody can catch that spirit and improve, be entrepreneurs, enjoy being here. Texas is so many things to so many people. I wear a cowboy hat and boots everyday. You don't have to do that to be a Texan. Texas is inside—not outside. There's so many things to like about it. People come here and they don't want to leave unless they get transferred or run out. And there's a reason for that. It's an intangible thing that you have to be here in order to experience. You stay here two or three years and you won't go anywhere. We got ya.

Be what you want to be. Texas let's you do that. That little underlying spirit means so much. You won't believe the difference in doing business here or living here as compared to somewhere else. There's something we've got that nobody else has. I don't know what that intangible is, but it's real. Intangible, but intrinsic—it gets into your psyche and you want to share it and talk about it. It's the spirit. You can tap it anytime you want. Texas, it moves you along like a current.

"Texas, Our Texas," the official state song of Texas, was adopted by the Texas Legislature in 1929. It was the winning entry of a contest.

SCOTT RYLANDER

★ BIRTHPLACE ★
Brazoria County near Freeport, TX

★ CURRENT RESIDENCE ★
Austin, TX

★ OCCUPATION ★
Corporate Trainer

*We close with an interview done very early in the process. This was the first
of several fifth generation or earlier Texans I managed to find. We had a long
conversation. Frankly, I wished it had gone even longer. It became the blueprint for
conducting the project. As you will see, he was so articulate and he touched on several
important concepts that get to the core of being Texan. I remember coming away from this
meeting knowing I was on to something worth pursuing. Listen closely as several concepts
come together. We began by asking what was so special about Texas.*

There are two things that make Texas special. It's the scale of the land itself and the people. If you go from the Piney Woods of East Texas—which although not a rainforest, they do get their share of the wet stuff—and then drive 20 hours to the west, you're in the middle of the northern edge of the Chihuahuan Desert. The Piney woods are relatively flat with some rolling hills and you've got the mountains out in West Texas. The Panhandle is as flat as a table and the Coastal Plain and the Hill Country are in the middle.

Look at Dallas versus Houston, or Austin versus San Antonio—and the types of people who not only have grown up there but the types who have been attracted to each of those cities. And that is just in modern times. In the history of the state itself, there's the Anglo settlements where you have the whites coming over from mostly the southern United States—the Deep South—who brought with them their slaves. Therefore you have African influence along with the Deep South influence.

Then there are the Germans who settled in the Hill Country and the Spanish who had lived there for years. The French influence you find on the coast from the LaSalle period, and then on up to today with Vietnamese and other Asian shrimpers.

You see it in stuff as simple as food, like Tex-Mex, for example. Well, what is it? It's kind of smashed together Deep South, Spanish and European tradition all being fed by the fact that you have cattle all over the place. As a result you get a brand new culinary design. These are the traditions that the people just accept as normal. We don't think of it as weird to have grown up speaking English, knowing a decent handful of Spanish, and having friends whose parents speak nothing but Spanish. To us that's just as normal as can be.

Just think of the people who live in East Texas, West Texas, the Panhandle, the big cities, the Rio Grande Valley and the Hill Country. If you live here long enough, in twenty seconds you know what part of the state they came from when they open their mouth. It's the scale of the land itself and the scale of the people that have driven that kind of diversity. Yet, it is the cooperation amongst all the groups that makes us what we are.

A lot of our independence and individuality is bred from our past, especially the period around and leading up to the Texas Revolution itself. Every other state in the Union—even the Republic itself has a history. Texas has a story. What I mean by the difference is that history is a list of facts with dates attached to them. But a story is something you tell because it's entertaining. If you took Texas history like everyone did in eighth grade, it was different than the Texas history that my Dad took and it's different from the Texas history that one of my college buddies is teaching in junior high right now. Because it is a story, it is constantly evolving. As new facts come to light, the story changes. Old facts turn out to maybe not be facts but just a damn good story. A lot of us latch onto stuff like the line drawn in the sand at the Alamo, the Black Bean incident, the routing of the Mexican Army at San Jacinto and the Alamo itself.

The folks that did come here had to bust their tails to make a living. For example, here in Austin, Texas, if you dig down six inches or so you'll hit solid limestone. This stuff is tough to farm. So there is a kind of independent spirit that is bred out of necessity. We don't have to worry about it much these days—after all, I can go to the

You can't tire of anything in this state 'cause if you get tired of something all you have to do is pick up and move about 200 miles away and you'll find something completely different.

local grocery store and not worry about how deep the topsoil is. But because I heard that story and it touched my heart, I took on that spirit, that sense of independence. It's a little bit of pride mixed in with a little bit of braggadocio because it's a good story.

For better or worse, the fact that you had to fight to live where you lived, and fight for your independence from a corrupt dictatorship back in Mexico, and that you have all the names and characters like Crockett, Travis, Bowie, Lamar, Houston, you couldn't write a better story. These characters are real folks and they're part of this real story. They are people you can really identify with and want to identify with and align yourself with because, just by association, it makes you look better.

I wouldn't want to limit the Texan persona to just the War for Independence. Look at West Texans ranching in the Big Bend country—that's a tough job. Then there's the Wildcatters and if you look at today, the people building Austin, Silicon Hills. They're the folks building the new economy. They have the same kind of attitude.

Being a Texan means you've got to have awareness and a pride of the past history and the story of the state. Anybody can be proud of the story but the key to being a Texan, and the most important part, is that you've got to feel a sense of responsibility to carry on and follow in the footsteps of the examples set by those characters in that story—not necessarily do the things they did. There's really no need to go invade Mexico—but...

I feel that I should follow their example, that I should be independent minded, try not to rely on other people, I should turn to myself for help first, but I should always be ready to offer help and render assistance as necessary. And I should be willing to do tough things if it's the right thing to do. To me, that's what it means to be a Texan right there.

People who have never lived in the United States know Texas. You can plop down in a Karaoke bar in Japan and soon the conversation turns to "where are you from?" Someone says, "Rhode Island. Oh, that's nice. I hear it is quite pretty in the fall. Where are you from? Texas. Oh wow, a Texan." You can draw the shape of Texas on a napkin and they'll recognize it.

Texas has an image or mystique—the Old West or whatever. Legitimately speaking, it was its own country for a decade, flew it's own flag and did it's own thing. It entered The Union under treaty and not the usual method of annexation.

One of my personal favorite places in the whole state is the Big Bend region— the Trans-Pecos—far West Texas. I heard it described once as the place where all the lies you ever heard about Texas are true. And it is one of the better descriptions of that particular area I have ever heard because most people think of Texas as a dusty, windblown desert with tumbleweeds, big ranches and stuff like that. That's not the case for all of the state, but out there it is. You are in the desert. To me, it's absolutely beautiful. I love the scale, just the sheer vastness of it all. The Spanish used to call it *el despoblado*— the unpeopled—because there's nothing out there. There were no native tribes that lived out there. There were some that would migrate through on

their way to other places and only small pockets of them stayed. The size, the silence, the scenery: The surroundings out there can swallow you up, but in a good way. That's where you realize what they mean when they say, "Everything is bigger in Texas." This is what they mean when they talk about people from Texas being friendly. It is out of necessity.

You can't tire of anything in this state 'cause if you get tired of something all you have to do is pick up and move about 200 miles away and you'll find something completely different.

Where else do you find people like me? Look at my ring—it's a representation of the state seal. I also have this tattoo right here, permanently. You probably don't find that too much in many other states, I wouldn't imagine. I could be wrong, but you don't see too many Wyoming tattoos.

The state's official flower is the Bluebonnet.

End of the Trail

I did not embark on this project with any preconceived notions on its outcome or what I would learn from the interviews. I'm a believer in "just do the work," so I trusted that concept and let the book reveal what I should know about Texas.

As I approached the end of the interview process, I realized the book was speaking to me. The interviews began to unveil several consistent themes. As different as these people's backgrounds and thought processes were, their traits, outlooks, and conclusions were similar, even though most of them did not know each other. It was the payoff I had hoped would emerge as the work progressed. It became obvious Texans share an intricate canvas of heritage, history, education, and tradition that goes toward defining the Texan character.

The Romantic Era of the nineteenth century was a time of idealism and romanticism. The style of the time was adopted by some of Texas' early historians. Glowing, if not idealistic, reports were articulated as fact. Granted, the perceptions might have been rooted in fact, but there was plenty of fancy injected in the observations, too. Each writer had a purpose or an agenda for what they wrote, some for economic gain, some for political expediency, and others simply had an axe to grind.

From the outset, the descriptions of Texas bordered on the grandiose. What was there not to believe? Texas offered seemingly endless tracts of land and wild game. The area bristled with opportunities for those daring enough to grasp them. These descriptions were much like Texas itself...bigger than life. People came here for the opportunity, not always aware of the struggle that most certainly would follow. These adventurers and pioneers were idealistic, determined and would not be denied.

The history of Texas is rife with individuals looking for second chances—people running from some kind of trouble, be it financial, political or domestic woes, even criminal prosecution. What they shared was a desire to start over—another chance to cash in on a dream.

Since opportunity has always existed in Texas, some were able to make their dreams payoff. Cows changed the economy of Texas and the cattle industry placed its indelible signature on the state. The cattle industry boomed and flourished. Self-made cattle barons created huge ranches—the XIT, the Waggoner, and the King spreads, covered territory larger than some states. The XIT at one point had over 6,000 miles of fence around one ranch that covered most of the western length of the Texas panhandle. A visit there reveals fresh images of the days when cowboys drove thousands of cattle up the trails to the railheads and the seemly ever-present Indian wars are indelibly etched into ones psyche as well.

Real cowboys still exist in Texas. Still doing what they've done for over 150 years. The hard physical work of tending to their herds still has to be done. Granted, technology has changed the way they approach many of the tasks they perform now a days, but ultimately, it often comes down to one man on horseback tending to one cow.

The cattle were the precursor of an even more lucrative industry—oil—a rough

Real cowboys still exist in Texas.

and tumble existence rife with uncertainties and danger. Wildcatters and roughnecks, the new cowboys, brought in oil wells throughout the state. It has often been said, "When Texas discovered oil, Texas changed the world." There is a lot of truth in that statement. To this day, cattle and oil are still vital and viable industries enhancing Texas' wealth and identity. Texans are fiercely proud of that heritage. Their pride is not merely bravado, they live what they believe. Several factors shape the Texan mindset.

Much of Texas pride comes from the fact that Texas was once its own country. No other state in the Union can make that claim and while Texans don't wear it on their sleeve, it is a part of their psyche and abundant pride. Sometimes you hear that Hawaii was a country too, however, Hawaii wasn't really a country. It was a constitutional monarchy that became a territory. Texas is also the only state to come into the Union by way of a treaty. Because of the unique circumstances of Texas' history, she was granted special rights and privileges. For one, her flag can fly at the same height as the American flag—a tribute to her former nation status.

When Texas joined the Union, it also reserved the right to divide itself into five different states, with one required to be named "Texas." The advantage of such an arrangement is that such a parceling could give the area of present day Texas ten senators in the U.S. Senate. Although the possibility of this ever happening is remote, don't put it out of the realm of possibility for some future politicians to make the case for carrying out such a scheme. In the past, schemes for dividing into as little as two states and as many as four were actively pursued. Obviously, each attempt failed to gain acceptance. One of the running jokes in Texas is that the reason that has never happened is that each area wanted to claim the name "Texas" and wouldn't give in to be named anything else. If that is the case, count on the impasse to last for generations.

The Republic of Texas stood on its own for nearly a decade and its descendants are acutely aware of the sacrifice and the rugged, independent pioneer spirit, of their predecessors. This most likely is the source of their fierce can-do attitude, that look-you-straight-in-the-eye confidence. If you want to get something done, tell a Texan it can't be done—then stand back.

Freedom and sacrifice are a part of Texas history and this also resonates within the Texas spirit as though they know their heritage has somehow "cut them from the herd." Being a sovereign nation sets Texas apart from her 49 sister states. Texans don't believe they're special—they know it.

Texas has always been about opportunity and the struggle that goes with it. Texas has always been a tough place to live. The original settlers had to fight the Indians, the land, the weather, the Mexicans, and often, each other just to survive. You had to earn the right to

live here. You earned it by surviving. Few things came easy to the early Texans. Perhaps, that is where some of the Texas spirit comes from. They are a proud bunch—some even say arrogant. Yet as tough as they are, most will often give you the shirt off their back without your asking.

The population of Texas has exploded over the past 30 years or so. More and more people have moved to the Lone Star State seeking opportunities just as generations before them have done. The influx does concern many native or long term Texans who believe there is a real danger of dilution or the outright loss of the Texas traditions, but one reason folks keep coming to Texas is the warmth of her people. Even though Texas has a colorful and storied past, Texans continue to welcome strangers with open arms. Once you move to Texas, you're considered a Texan. It's really just that simple.

Texans appreciate people who will look them straight in the eye and offer them a firm handshake. Although friendly, you don't want to cross them. Once you violate their trust, you're done— might as well find another place to be. You're not likely to get a second chance to fool 'em again. They're quick learners that way.

While welcoming, they also expect you to assimilate into the culture. Often new residents come to Texas, understandably, with their own traditions and values. The problems arise when the newcomers try to change Texas into the place they left. This is nothing new.

Ironically, the same sort of situation was present when all those Texans came here in the 1820s and '30s.

From a very early age, Texans are exposed, if not immersed, in Texas History. Texas is one of the few states in the country where its state history is vigorously mandated by the state's department of education. This goes a long way to perpetuating the Texan's mindset. Texas History is taught in the fourth and again in the seventh grade. That is the law. Through their studies, youngsters begin to identify with Texan values and traditions. They grow up surrounded by everything Texas; therefore, it's a natural osmosis. The story is certainly easy for young minds to absorb and include as a part of their identity. Anyone wanting to graduate from a college in Texas, is most likely going to take a semester of Texas history or Texas government. Therefore, most kids grow up with a healthy respect for Texas, her traditions and her story. Ask anyone ten years old or older about the Alamo. Then, stand back and be impressed.

The education often continues at home, especially if the parents were raised in Texas. It's passed on from generation to generation. The story of Texas is a birthright. At some point, you realize you're a Texan and that somehow makes you different. Texas pride is a real entity and it is inherited, nurtured and crafted from generation to generation. The children of Texans are brought up listening to the histories and legends. Having talked with many fifth, sixth, and even seventh genera-

tion Texans, I found a simple similarity, the further back one's generations go in Texas history—the greater the sense of pride. One can't help but feel a palpable sense of entitlement. It's as though the deeper the generational roots reach into Texas' past the farther out the chest expands. For the most part, Texans completely buy into and reinforce the myths and legends that are the Texas image. None is held in higher regard than the Alamo. Texas fought for and gained its independence from Mexico. And Texas is still a place where independence and freedom are cherished and admired. Real people struggled, fought, shed blood and died for the land Texans revere today.

If there is a common house of worship in Texas, it is, without a doubt, the remains of an indefensible, broken down, old mission in San Antonio. It is the most cherished piece of ground in Texas. The Alamo is the shrine all Texans accept as the symbol of their hard won independence. The Alamo is the crucible of Texas liberty. It's a very real part of the Texas psyche. Texans quickly speak of the sacrifice that took place there followed by the unquestioned appreciation they have for the price paid. They may not dwell on it, but they certainly recognize its value to Texas' heritage and the role it played in the existence of Texas. It's a personal place even for those who have never been there. Every Texan we talked to, who mentioned the Alamo, spoke of it with reverence.

Why is the Alamo so powerful? Many scholarly works have already been

Ask anyone ten years old or older about the Alamo. Then stand back and be impressed.

written that address that question far beyond the scope of this book. In my opinion, after the Mexican Army, under General Cos, was driven from San Antonio at the Siege of Bexar in December of 1835, General Cos went back and told Santa Anna what happened. The dictator was not happy. He decided it was time to send a message to these upstart, ungrateful Texians and to make it clear they were no longer welcome.

His policy was nothing short of ethnic cleansing. His plan was to drive the Texians out of Texas. He figured if he killed enough of them, it would frighten the rest to leave Texas and go back to where they came from. Proof? He ordered all the prisoners to be executed at Goliad. Fortunately, some managed to escape. He ordered all the combatants at the Alamo to be slain, but he did allow some non-combatant survivors, like Susanna Dickenson and her daughter, to leave to act as witnesses and spread the word.

The men at the Alamo had chances to cut and run. They chose not to, even though they knew they were going to die. They were sacrificing their lives for a bigger cause. Although they all died, they served as an example of determination and courage. Santa Anna's plan backfired. The Texians didn't get scared,

they got mad. The Texians dug in their heels and won the day and independence at San Jacinto.

It is only an assumption on my part, but I believe that at least a portion of the Texan value system is rooted at that old mission. Texans still cherish and admire courage, freedom, individuality, and those who stand up for what they believe. You can sense it in the tone of their words. I have often wondered if they realize that they often emulate the values of those brave men who fought to the death. Science may not back it up but I'm convinced it's in their DNA. For Texans, it's as real as rain. Somehow, they are connected to the Alamo defenders at some spiritual level. They can't tell you how any better than I can, but I know they feel it to the core of their beings. The Alamo is a mighty special place.

There is one common misconception that is often stated as fact throughout Texas. Many interviewed for this book made the statement that Texas is still able to secede from the union. Well, that's not accurate. Back when Texas came into the United States under the original treaty, perhaps, a case could be made then for the argument. But then, the Civil War happened. Texas was not readmitted until five years after the Civil War and it was understood, if you come back into the Union, it was for good. In reality, any state could secede and the federal government really couldn't stop them other than slap economic sanctions and perhaps call up the Army. But when Texas rejoined the Union after the Civil War, like most Southern States, it was devastated and had a huge debt. It wasn't in a position to dictate many terms to the federal government. Once they rejoined the Union, they knew they were in it for keeps.

Make no mistake about it. The image of Texas did not just happen. It was created on purpose. Over the years, it has gained an inertia of its own. From time to time, the image gets worked and reworked by various circles of influence. But nothing has ever diminished Texas' Western, bigger-n-life stature. How it all happened is probably as interesting a story ever told about Texas.

You might think the image making goes back to the early Texas historians. You would be right to a degree. They certainly glorified the many attributes of Texas that aligned with their self-interests. But if you really wanted to put a date on the birth of the Texas image, you need to go back to October 1910.In the 1890s, there were groups that had been making efforts to create more interest in the Texas Revolution Era. This was the period when Elizabeth Ney was commissioned to sculpt the statues of Stephen F. Austin and Sam

> But nothing has ever diminished Texas' Western, bigger-n-life stature.

Houston. Gaining interest and financial support was difficult. The statues were finally unveiled in 1903. The copies appear at the south entrance of the Rotunda at the Texas Capitol building. During this period, there was a rebirth of Texas history. Until this time, the events and people of the Texas Revolution Era were widely ignored and perhaps, not thought of as anything particularly important. They were simply events that happened. Then Governor Thomas M. Campbell, and the soon to be Governor, Oscar Branch Colquitt, and others saw the need and an opportunity to change that perception.

Right after the turn of the new century, the nation was immersed in a movement known as the Progressive Era. It was a time for looking forward and embracing anything and everything "modern." Only three decades earlier, Texas had come through the Civil War on the losing side and was readmitted the United States in 1870. As the Progressive Era was beginning to take hold in the early Twentieth century, Texas was beginning to embrace the persona of the West and, an American image as well.

Texas wanted to distance itself from all the nastiness associated with the Civil War, slavery and the "Lost Cause." Texas was consciously seeking to change its image and display itself in a more positive light. The question was asked, "What usable history do we have?" Well, there was this matter of a revolution for independence and a time when Texas was its own country. This was something to build a new future upon.

In October of 1910, the Texas legislature passed a bill to exhume the body of Stephen F. Austin from his resting place of 74 years on his sister's plantation at Peach Point and move him to the Texas State Cemetery in Austin. On October 18, he was exhumed and brought to Brazoria where a memorial service was held for the "Father of Texas." School children were let out of school so they could participate in the memorial. Each child was given a flower to place upon the casket as they passed in a solemn procession. The body, transported by train, continued its journey toward Austin.

When the train made its next stop in Angleton, the local children participated in a similar ceremony. The next memorial was held in Houston. Again, the children played a central role. In addition to the flower ceremonies, they sang "America" and "The Texas Flag Song." The final event, which took place in Austin, lasted three days. Again, children played a prominent role. They formed a line along each side of that long promenade on the south side of the Capitol grounds as the casket was carried out of the building. The Father of Texas was solemnly carried between the rows of children down the long walkway and then eventually to his final resting place at the Texas State Cemetery and then laid to rest.

Having the children involved at such a visible level was anything but a coincidence. It was a deliberate, disarmingly simple strategy. If you allow the children to participate in something of historical significance, they will remember it for the rest of their lives. They will tell their children and grandchildren of their place in history. The generational passing of the story had begun.

This was a time when other Texas heroes were reinterred at the Texas State Cemetery and statues were erected. It was also the first time since the battle in 1836 that serious efforts to save the Alamo grounds were initiated. Since the battle, the structure had been turned into everything from an army post, a police station, a liquor store, and a general store. More about these events in Texas history can be found in Gregg Cantrell's wonderful article in Southwestern Historical Quarterly, October 2004 entitled, "Stephen F. Austin's Bones." You will begin to understand how the "Texas Attitude" was, in a sense, manufactured. It signifies the birth of the Marketing of Texas. The process has continued non-stop ever since.

Texas' image has often been shaped and exploited by the media— Hollywood, radio and television. The dime novels and pulp books found huge acceptance throughout the country in the late nineteenth century. These quickly produced paperbacks made for fanciful and exciting reading. Many of the Texas legends and myths were born out of this process. In countless movies and TV shows, images and

I may not have found the T-Chromosome but I do know that it exists. It is as real as the Alamo, the land and that big Texas sky.

perceptions supposedly representing Texas, have been loosely fed to the masses since Thomas Edison invented the motion picture. The entertainment media has seldom let facts get in the way of a good story. In fact, one of the first movies ever produced was a "Western." In 1903, the first "western", The Great Train Robbery, was filmed near Dover, New Jersey. So it would appear, they've been getting it wrong from the git-go.

One of my favorite absurdities was watching the good guy with the white hat chasing the bad guys with guns blazing through endless acres of Saguaro cactus. That species of cactus only grows in Arizona...two states away from Texas! Then there were the stagecoach chases through Monument Valley, which happens to be in Arizona and Utah, but it was supposed to be Texas. As much as I enjoyed watching JR on "Dallas," can you imagine what people in Europe, Asia or Africa, must think of us after watching all those reruns? It's amazing how a grain of truth becomes gospel.

So, why are Texans the way they are? First of all, they can't help it. Often, they can't tell you why they are the way they are. They live their lives to the fullest and rarely feel like they've been cheated. Texans make the most of their opportunities. They think big and act accordingly, and closely associate themselves with the concept of Texas once being its own country. They learned about it at school and at home. They connect with the events at the Alamo, and therefore, understand freedom, sacrifice, courage, and being fiercely individual. They cherish the notion of being connected to all that.

Does this describe every Texan? Certainly not. Yet in the case of the people we talked to for this book, these were the common traits. This book was never intended to be a scientific, sociological study of quantifiable Texaness. It was simply an act of curiosity.

This search reminds me of something on a poster I owned when I was a kid.

T. S. Eliot said it:

We shall never cease from exploration
And the end of all our exploring
Will be to arrive where we started
And know the place for the first time.

That's really what happened for me. I'm satisfied. I may not have found the T-Chromosome, but I do know that it exists. It is as real as the Alamo, the land and that big Texas sky.

Two words have been constant through-out this work. Pride and People. If the participants didn't actually say the words, it was clear that was what they were talking about. If you're new to Texas, just kick back and roll with the flow. Before long, you'll be acting and thinking like a Texan. You'll fit in just fine. Just don't try to change the rest of us.

Unlike my wife and son, I was not born in Texas. None of us get to choose the place for that event. However, I do get to choose where I live. I'm home. I have a window sticker of the Texas flag with the word underneath that simply says "HOME," period. That says it all.

Texas is a wonderful place where people have a strong belief in God and Friday night football is a religion. It is a place where possibilities are limited only by your capacity to dream—a place where dreams do come true if you are willing to work hard enough to achieve them.

Texans wear their pride like an extra layer of skin. You can't see it, but it is visible. Just watch how they carry themselves. You couldn't ask for better friends or neighbors. Texas is very per-sonal and doesn't mean exactly the same thing for any two people. In many ways, it is still its own country. A palpa-ble nationalism still thrives in Texas. Yes, we're all Americans, but for many we're Texans first. For us, Texas is more than a geographical location. Texans know it's located at the intersection of their heart and soul.

~ ❧ ~

Adios!

Recommended Reading

Sketches from the Five States of Texas, by A. C. Greene, Texas A&M Press

Lone Star, by T. R. Fehrenbach, Da Capo Press

Inventing Texas, Laura Lyons McLemore, Texas A&M Press

Texan Iliad, by Stephen L. Hardin, University of Texas Press

Goodbye to a River, by John Graves, Alfred A. Knopf

The Time It Never Rained, by Elmer Kelton, TCU Press
(and anything else by Elmer Kelton)

Anything written by J. Frank Dobie, University of Texas Press.

Texas Curiosities: Quirky Characters, Roadside Oddities and Other Offbeat Stuff,
by John Kelso, Globe Pequot

Titles by Susie Kelly Flatau:
Quotable Texas Women
Historic Texas Depots.
Counter Culture Texas,
From My Mother's Hands,
Red Boots & Attitude
Reaching Out to Today's Kids.

Things to Talk About

* What do suppose would have happened if Texas had decided not to rejoin the United States following the Civil War?

* What does it mean to you personally to be a native Texan?

* At what point in your life did you realize that you were a Texan?
  When and how did you realize being a Texan somehow made you different?

* What do you consider to be Texas traits?

* What Texan traits do find within your own community that defines your own Texaness?

* People often comment on the friendliness of Texans. Why do you think Texans are so welcoming?

* What makes Texas special and unlike any place else?

* What do you like most about living in Texas and being Texan?